FAMILY THERAPY AND SIBLING POSITION

WALTER TOMAN, Ph.D

Translated by Walter Toman, Ph.D.

WITHDRAWN

Jason Aronson Inc.
Northvale, New Jersey
London

Originally published as *Familientherapie: Grundlagen,
empirische Erkenntnisse und Praxis.*
© 1979 Wissenschaftliche Buchgesellschaft, Darmstadt.

10 9 8 7 6 5 4 3 2 1

Library of Congress Cataloging-in-Publication Data

Toman, Walter.
  Family therapy and sibling position.

  Translation of: Familientherapie.
  Bibliography: p.
  Includes index.
  1. Family psychotherapy. 2. Birth order. I. Title.
RC488.5.T6513 1988   616.89′156   87-33664
ISBN 0-87668-966-7

Manufactured in the United States of America.

To my family

CONTENTS

PREFACE

The present book is an English translation and expansion of the book I originally published in German in 1979. It is the outgrowth of my psychotherapeutic and research work started in Europe in the early fifties and carried on in the United States and Europe ever since, and of my teaching clinical psychology and psychotherapy for more than thirty years. Reviewers of the German book have emphasized its comprehensive base of empirical data, its solid roots in classical psychotherapy, and its didactic merits. I hope American and other English-speaking readers will find the book useful.

Walter Toman

ACKNOWLEDGMENTS

My special thanks go to those good and dedicated people who helped with the English manuscript. In chronological order they are: Christel Schander, who typed and corrected it in her spare moments at our Institute of Psychology at the University of Erlangen-Nürnberg; Peter Hough of the Language Laboratory of our University, who subtly and decisively improved the English; Dr. Jason Aronson of Northvale, New Jersey, my publisher; and Elena Le Pera, editor, who thoughtfully and painstakingly worked to get the manuscript into its final form for the North American reader.

Without those four friends and, of course, without the challenges of my colleagues, students, and patients, there would be no such book. Thanks again.

Walter Toman

1

THE DEVELOPMENT OF PSYCHOTHERAPY

A ttempts to help people with their emotional problems and pains have been known since ancient times. Rejection in love, unhappiness, or jealousy among the powerful and rich, worry about the passing of life, or the disobedience of one's children has through the centuries made men and women seek counsel and comfort from their elders, wise men, priests, and later from their philosophers.

Some of the emotional problems and pains, however, have been too severe for these counselors. Some people were desperate, in panic, or confused. They could not tell dreams from reality. They raged against their families, attacked people, property, goods, and livestock. Often they hurt themselves in the process and were considered possessed by devils or demons. In fact, in order to protect society from those so badly stricken, they were chased away, locked up in towers, or even killed. In The Middle Ages, such persons were often accused of witchcraft. A medieval book, *The Witches' Hammer or Malleus Maleficorum* (Institoris and Sprenger 1487) reported on the art of proving witchcraft through torture.

Even at that time there were more humane observers who argued against the assumed complicity with the devil of which the "witches" were accused. Rather they were sick people with mental problems who required protection (Vives 1492–1540 and Weyer 1515–1588, quoted from Zilboorg and Henry 1941). Other humanists followed suit (Dix 1802–1887, Pinel 1745–1826, and Charcot 1825–1893, quoted from Zilboorg and Henry 1941), and by the eighteenth century even ordinary people were more willing to tolerate mental illness. This better public understanding of psychological disturbances had been furthered by great poets like Shakespeare, Molière, and Goethe, who explored madness in their plays and dramatized how some of their heroes had become crazy. It also helped that some of the great poets, composers, and painters had themselves developed severe psychological disturbances. Scientific observers had begun to trace the growth of their illness in the thoughts and work of these artists.

In the nineteenth century psychiatrists succeeded in ordering mental illness by type and severity. They distinguished *cognitive* from *emotional* disorders and separated them from other mental afflictions (Kraepelin 1883). The latter included illnesses like general paresis — which Haslam and Esquirol were able to separate from early dementia or schizophrenia on the one hand and mania and depression on the other and which Fournier and von Krafft-Ebing were able to link up with preceding syphilitic infections (Zilboorg and Henry 1941) — along with nervous states of lesser severity such as neurotic illness or *neuroses*.

Like cognitive and emotional disorders, neuroses seemed to have no identifiable physical basis. There were hunches that cognitive psychoses (such as schizophrenia, hebephrenia, and paranoia) and emotional psychoses (such as mania and depression, or the "divine affliction" epilepsy), had physiological origins. Physiological treatments such as insulin shock, electroshock, barbiturates, and other psychogenic stimulants and depressants were tried with considerable success. The neuroses, on the other hand, were considered psychological in origin. Traumatic experiences and hard-to-change life situations laden with frustration and conflict were seen as the causes (e.g., by Janet 1892, Charcot 1886–1890, and Freud 1894, 1900, 1916–1917). Hence, other courses of treatment were tried: suggestion, hypnosis, and finally psychoanalysis and psychoanalytic therapy.

CLASSICAL PSYCHOTHERAPY

Freud's rejection of suggestion and hypnosis in favor of the method of psychoanalysis may be considered a turning point in history. Like Socrates, who involved his discussants not so much in lectures on the world, man, or ethics, as he did in the expression and development of their own thoughts about these issues and in the ambiguities and contradictions that emerged in the process, Freud requested his patients to utter whatever came to mind regardless of whether it seemed smart or dumb, good or evil, joyous, frightening, or annoying. The psychoanalyst observed and listened, questioned, commented on, and interpreted the patients' thoughts, ideas, and memories along with their implicit affects and conflicts; but as a person the analyst stayed in the background. Freud's own wishes and memories were of no concern. The psychoanalyst remained in a state of neutrality toward the patient. He told him nothing, and gave no instructions. He offered no material help in the patient's daily life and refrained from giving advice or orders. He merely helped the patient explore himself and his past and, through his own insight and at his discretion, to reappraise and rearrange his life. The psychoanalyst helped the patient to help himself.

Freud discovered that it was not easy for patients to say everything that came to mind. They often halted and sometimes felt uncomfortable enough to stop the treatment. Freud described those phenomena as *inner resistances* of patients against unconscious or repressed motives and affects. They may have been afraid to express their hatred of a particular person. They may have avoided the memory of a festive event, perhaps because of some major disappointment experienced there. Patients may be overcome by sad feelings and unable to tell why; in fact, nothing at all may come to mind. Freud observed, moreover, that in spite of the psychotherapist's self-restraint and his affective neutrality, patients sometimes felt hated or despised, and at other times appreciated, loved, or feared by the therapist. They also experienced feelings of warmth or annoyance, of love, admiration, fear, sorrow, or envy toward the therapist. If the therapist had given patients no occasion for such feelings— as required by the rules of conduct of psychotherapy—they were apparently responding to the therapist in ways that in their own past had been evoked by people who had been important to them. Freud called this phenomenon *transference*. Patients involuntarily transferred or projected their feelings onto the therapist.

Steady observation and occasional responses to patients' transference behavior is an important part of the task of the psychoanalyst or psychoanalytically oriented therapist. Psychoanalytic therapy—which, as we mentioned, resembles the Socratic art of philosophical discussion—has also been called *classical psychotherapy*. In contrast to philosophical discussion, however, psychotherapeutic dialogue does not concern itself so much with enlightened views of humanity and the world as with patients' affects, motives, and interests governing daily life. What they want from life, what they cannot get or think they cannot get, what scares, annoys, or depresses them is the subject of discussion. The psychotherapist helps patients to recover supposedly lost opportunities to realize goals and interests or, if these turn out to be unavailable in reality after all, to renounce them more successfully than before.

The topics of dialogue are chosen by patients, but the therapist may come back to any topic already mentioned by them. The therapist comments and interprets the expressions of patients and takes note of signs of possible inner resistances as well as of transference.

The beginning of classical psychotherapy dates back to the turn of this century. Since then, however, it has been refined in various ways. Whereas patients' inner resistances had originally been dealt with by "frontal attack," psychotherapists increasingly learned how to circumvent resistances and use their soft spots. Thus psychotherapy became less shocking for the patients and ultimately more successful. It happened less and less often that patients would rather give up psychotherapy than their inner resistances. Transference was no longer characterized by fear and awe as it had been in the early years of classical psychotherapy.

Classical psychotherapy, however, is not merely Freudian therapy. Jung (1912), Adler (1920), and their disciples must also be subsumed under classical psychotherapy. It does not matter that Jung and Adler, Sullivan (1947) or Schultz-Hencke (1940, 1951), had slightly different guidelines for choosing among patients' topics. Classical psychotherapy can even be considered the mother-matrix of those schools of psychotherapy that eventually departed from it in favor of different types of psychotherapeutic intervention, such as nondirective or client-centered therapy, behavior therapy, and communication therapy.

Classical therapy is not restricted to individual therapy.

In psychotherapy with children, with groups, and with families, rules of psychotherapeutic intervention are about the same except for modifications due to the specific context. In child psychotherapy there is playing as well as talking; a certain inventory of toys belongs to the child therapist's equipment. In group psychotherapy *all* members are supposed to say what comes into their minds. Consideration of others and their wishes is necessary. Not only the group therapist but the group members, too, must listen and let others finish. In addition to transference of each group member's feelings, motives, and conflicts onto the therapist, there is transference onto other group members that requires the therapist's attention. In family therapy the therapist has to keep an eye on chronic transferences that family members have cast upon each other. A father may have the wish that his son take care of him like a big brother or that his daughter forever stay a little girl. A mother may hope that her son will one day make up for the suffering caused by her unloving husband. A daughter may plan on dealing with her mother the way she saw the mother deal with her parents.

OTHER SCHOOLS OF PSYCHOTHERAPY

Nondirective or Client-centered Therapy

Rogers (1942) developed *nondirective therapy* in the early forties, partly in protest against the supposed interpretation mania of psychoanalysts, especially when it came to dealing with the inner resistances of patients. The psychoanalyst apparently could never be wrong. When he contended that a woman patient, for instance, hated her mother and wanted to be with her divorced father, the patient could either acknowledge that those were indeed her feelings—coupled, say, with feelings of guilt over betraying her mother—or

deny that she had such feelings: She actually hated her
father and was, if anything, too dependent on her mother.
Yet in the eyes of the psychoanalyst she was merely resisting
his interpretation (see also Haley 1963).

As in classical psychotherapy, Rogers let the patient say
whatever he wanted, but he did not deem the patient's past
or his supposed transference behavior important. What
mattered to Rogers was the patient's feelings at the present
time. If the therapist constantly reflected what he heard the
patient saying—submitting it to the patient for approval, as it
were, as a check on rendering accurately the patient's
feelings—and if the therapist offered the patient an attitude
of unconditional acceptance, transference behavior would
not even occur (Rogers 1951).

We shall see that transference behavior can hardly be
prevented, and Rogers, by demanding that the psychotherapist accept the patient unconditionally, is actually extracting
transference behavior from the therapist—or rather, according to Freud, countertransference behavior—and pro-
voking a certain kind of transference in the patient. The
patient should experience the therapist as a kind, motherly
person who is imposing no constraints.

Rogers called his form of therapy *patient-* or *client-
centered* (Rogers 1951), apparently implying that other forms
of psychotherapy were not patient- or client-centered. Roge-
rians in Germany even called it *dialogue therapy*, as if other
forms of psychotherapy were not based on dialogue.

Behavior Therapy

Behavior therapy can be viewed as an attempt to adjust and
utilize learning theory in psychotherapy (Bandura 1969,
Blöschl 1969, Dollard and Miller 1950, Eysenck 1964, Lazarus
1971, London 1972, Meyer and Chesser 1970, Mowrer 1950,

Wolpe 1958). There are three basic methods in behavior therapy.

The first one has been called *reciprocal inhibition* (also, *anxiety inhibition* or desensitization). Patients are encouraged and helped by the therapist to tolerate increasingly intensive versions of those stimuli or fantasies that they are afraid of in reality. It is hoped that such laboratory practices will enable patients to eventually confront those experiences, events, and persons that are causing their fears and that their successes in overcoming those fears will grow.

The second method has been called *aversion training*. The therapist discourages the patients' persistent undesirable behavior, such as bedwetting or transvestitism (the tendency of a man to dress up as a woman and vice versa), by disapproving or scolding, by administering exercises in visualizing unpleasant consequences, and even by inflicting physical pain.

The third method is what behavior therapists call *imitation-, observation-, or model-learning*. The therapist presents the patient with examples of persons who do what the patient is afraid of or what he wants—or is urged—to avoid. Sometimes the behavior therapist shows the patient what to do.

Of these three methods, the first derives from classical psychotherapy. The classical therapist also helps patients to reduce their fears of experiences and persons that are no longer realistic (although they probably were at an earlier time). In classical therapy, however, this procedure is much freer and more complicated and is conducted at a pace set by the patients themselves. The psychotherapist gives no orders, actively introduces no exercises, but rather accompanies patients attentively with his thoughts, memories, and affective responses.

There is no aversion training in classical psychotherapy. The hope is that the patient, while discovering opportunities to fulfill goals and realize interests that he had thought unobtainable, will lose the need to carry out undesirable behavior. It becomes less satisfying than the newly discovered or rediscovered opportunities.

Finally, observation-, model-, or imitation-learning plays only an indirect part in classical psychotherapy. The classical therapist helps the patient to explore the model persons of his past and present everyday life, their importance to him, the usefulness of their messages, and the patient's thoughts of them. The classical therapist does not show patients how to do things; he does not teach or instruct them. The only example that the classical therapist does give patients is his handling of their affects, motives, and conflicts. In the course of treatment patients are increasingly learning how to view themselves the way the psychotherapist views them. They are gradually and implicitly learning to anticipate the questions, comments, and interpretations of the therapist. Ultimately, they will be able to produce similar interpretations. The more often patients succeed in doing that without intending or contriving to do it, the closer they probably are to ending psychotherapeutic treatment. Soon they will need the therapist no longer.

Communication Therapy

Communication therapists are not so much interested in changing or healing psychologically disturbed persons as they are in correcting and improving inadequate communications between them and other people (Bateson et al. 1956, Laing et al. 1966, Watzlawick et al. 1967). Such improvements, they claim, will automatically result in reducing the psychological disturbance. The theory is that psychological disorder has originated from ambiguous or contradictory communications coming from important persons in one's life, especially from parents. Those communications must be spotted, clarified in their implications, and changed.

Classical psychotherapy operates on similar assumptions. Here, too, relations with others are to be changed and improved. All external conflicts, it is assumed, have been generated in dealing with others. All internal or inner conflicts of a person stem from external and real conflicts. Anxieties, aggressions, and renunciations brought about during a person's development predominantly concern people in his or her immediate environment.

Communication therapy differs from classical psychotherapy in that it tries to improve the language by which patients communicate with persons important to them or with group members in group therapy. Nonverbal or implicit communications are considered too, but the treatment itself is mostly verbal and logical, and it focuses on current patterns of communication. Thus, patients learn to express themselves more clearly; under the therapist's guidance they practice communicating without ambiguities or contradictions. Sometimes patients adopt the concepts and premises of communication theory.

Classical psychotherapy does not ordinarily offer such instructions. The psychotherapist primarily uses the patient's expressions and idioms. He introduces no theoretical concepts or scientific discourse. Patients do not so much resolve the logical contradictions in their dealings with others and with the environment as they do their emotional experiences and practical or even physical conflicts of interest (Pongratz 1973, 1978, Schraml 1970, Toman 1968, 1978a, b).

NEWER FORMS OF PSYCHOTHERAPY

Besides these larger schools of psychotherapy, of which communication therapy is the youngest and hence, the one with the smallest stock of experience, there are other lesser schools. The more interesting ones among them will be briefly mentioned.

Freud's method of treatment before he tried psychoanalysis was hypnosis. *Hypnotherapy* (Wolberg 1948) continues this tradition. *Rational therapy* (Ellis 1950) emphasizes logical consistency of the patients' thoughts and opinions in their present reality even before communication therapy does. *Reality therapy* (Glasser 1965) follows suit, with special emphasis on clients' conflicts in making a living and avoiding jail.

Practical and emotional experience and the living through of conflicts during treatment is stressed by *emotive therapy* (Whitaker and Malone 1953). In *direct analysis* (Fromm-Reichmann 1950, Rosen 1953) the psychotherapist attempts to treat severely disturbed and psychotic patients by assuming the role of a protective maternal person. In that way the therapist can address himself even to the most primitive and infantile of patients' motives, make those motives more acceptable to the patient, and discuss them. In *gestalt therapy* (Perls 1973, Perls et al. 1951) situations and conflicts with present or past persons are reenacted in spatial and social paradigms. In *psychodrama* (Moreno 1946) patients are encouraged or directed to attempt conflict resolution by role playing with other persons.

In *transactional psychotherapy* (Berne 1964, Harris 1967) three levels of expression analogous to that of Freud's are distinguished: those of the infantile, the adult, and the parental ego. In their interactions two persons may generate misunderstandings and conflict by talking to each other on different levels. The transactional therapist tries to help people to communicate on identical levels.

In *autogenic training* (Schultz 1932) the patient is taught to gain better control over his own involuntary processes, particularly over muscle tonus, blood circulation, and breathing, and to influence them by auto-suggestion. In *catathymic imagery* (Leuner 1970) the therapist encourages patients to expand upon initial suggestions of certain situations and to describe what they see and experience. In *primal therapy* (Janov 1970) the catharsis of *primal pain*, that is, of the patient's earliest disappointments in life, is attempted by exercises in primal crying and screaming.

Existential therapy and *existential analysis* (Binswanger 1953, Caruso 1952, Frankl 1947, Jaspers 1946, May 1953, von Weizsäcker 1947 et al.) both attempt not only to recover opportunities for satisfaction in terms of motivation and interests that the patient believes lost—as does classical psychotherapy—but also to help the patient search for the meaning of life. If need be, the therapist is willing to teach the patient such meaning and even to refer him to religion and God. *Humanistic psychologists* (e.g., Angyal 1941, Bühler and Massarik 1968, Goldstein 1940, Kelly 1955, Mahrer 1967, Maslow 1954, Rogers 1951) pursue similar, if less metaphysical interests in their psychotherapies.

2

THE DEVELOPMENT OF FAMILY THERAPY

THE ORIGINS OF FAMILY THERAPY

Child psychotherapy deals with the conflicts of the child with one or both parents or with siblings, and sometimes with conflicts prevailing among the parents themselves. The child's attempts to live with such conflicts lead to conspicuous or neurotic behavior and eventually bring him or her to the therapist (see e.g., Axline 1947, Erikson 1950, A. Freud 1927, Klein 1932).

To the extent that children in play therapy dare to express themselves more freely as they experience tolerance and encouragement from the psychotherapist, they tend to change at home as well. This can upset the parents. A child turned shy and anxious because of a smoldering parental conflict may begin to feel and act more aggressively, may test his parents with increasing demands, and may eventually utter the crucial one: father should love mother, or at least be kind to her, and if he leaves the family he should pay heavily.

In such a case the *parents* usually need counseling as well. They have to learn in some fashion about the child's concern, but cannot expect the therapist to betray the confidences of the child either. The parents have to be prepared for the changes in behavior and feelings that the child may show in the course of treatment. If the parents get into their own troubles in the process, they may need psychotherapy. This, however, cannot be had from the same psychotherapist. The child would distrust the therapist, would want to know what the parents are telling him, and on whose side the therapist is himself. The parents would also have the same questions and doubts. Remaining the mediator between child and parents is, therefore, undeniably difficult.

One way out is to offer the parents another counselor or therapist, sometimes even two, so that each parent could have his or her confidant, and occasionally all three clients and their respective counselors would get together and discuss the situation. In that case, the counselors and therapists have to guard against revealing their clients' secrets. Even now they are not supposed to divulge anything that their clients had told them confidentially unless they get their explicit permission to do so. The safest way for the therapist is to let the client tell the others himself.

In view of those complications emerging in the conduct of child psychotherapy and counseling with parents and in view of the number of psychotherapists involved and their need to confer with each other, family therapy may have been in the making for the past fifty years. On the other hand, therapists have been hesitant to give up individual psychotherapy. Its clarity and dedication to patients' problems seemed hard to match.

As *group therapy* became more popular, courage to try family therapy grew. Group therapists had learned to listen to several group members at once or to the group as a whole while attending to the rules of classical psychotherapy (e.g., Aichhorn 1925, Ammon 1973, Balint 1957, Battegay 1967, Bion 1961, Foulkes 1974, Richter 1972, Slavson 1950, Yalom 1970). This necessitated that the group members, too, listen to each member who talked and that they let that person finish.

Transference behavior could be expected from each group member, not only with regard to the group therapist, but also to each of the group members. Transference behavior onto the therapist could differ from group member to group member. One of them wants the therapist to act like the strict and powerful father, another prefers him to be kind and tolerant, rather like a mother, and a third one suspects the therapist of making fun of him.

Countertransference behavior—that is, behavior or attitudes originating from still-unresolved current or old conflicts of the therapist himself—has sometimes been more successfully kept in check by these differential expectations of group members than in individual psychotherapy. If the group therapist fulfills the expectations of one group member, another one may feel disappointed and may protest. The group may stop talking, or hostility and strife may spring up among those members whose secret target is the therapist. Sooner or later the therapist will have to consider his countertransference behavior, talk about it, and even interpret it. At that point, he or she will have stopped being the group's optimal listener and will have burdened the group with a problem of his or her own. It is important to the group that the group leader admit to such an error of intervention when it occurs. It is even more important that the therapist commit the fewest possible such errors.

Transference behavior of group members onto other group members is a different matter. They need not respond with emotional neutrality and a reference to the perpetrator's past and everyday life, as the therapist does. They may respond with countertransference behavior as they would in reality. If somebody attacks them in everyday life, they may defend themselves or even counterattack. If somebody surprises them with an offer of warm affection, they could accept it, think it over, or reject it. They are under no obligation to explore a partner's reasons or the origin of his feelings in the past.

Since the rule of neutrality holds only for the group leader, he is no ordinary group member. Instead, he tries to guide group sessions in the interest of all group members and to stay in the background. He also determines when to end a session. Moreover, he is the organizer of the group. He selects group patients according to certain aspects and negotiates the terms of their participation. He may, for instance, assemble a group of mothers who have so far had only one child; perhaps he may include one or two mothers who have had more children. The mothers may be older or younger, working or not working, financially independent or in trouble. Their children may have been born weeks, months, or years ago.

In a group of students he may gather men and women from various schools and of various ages. In a group of physicians and social workers who want to talk about psychological problems they are having with their patients (Balint 1957), he may accept them under the provision that they don't know each other and are not working in the same place. Since a group should not be large (five to seven members is considered optimal), such a balanced selection of members is not always easy to accomplish.

A group leader usually rules that the group member may leave the group whenever he chooses as long as he has informed the group in advance and has given the group a chance to talk about it. The group leader may determine, moreover, that new members can enter only with the group's consent, or that members should not have contact with each other outside the group while therapy is still going on. He also suggests termination of treatment and calls the last session after the group has had an opportunity to discuss his proposal to terminate and its implications.

One of the remarkable advantages of group therapy is the opportunity of group members to learn how other group members are handling life situations and conflicts and to take them as models. A group leader following principles of classical group therapy, however (as in classical individual psychotherapy), will tend to say nothing about himself, will not dispense advice, nor will the therapist indicate how he or she would deal with the particular situation or conflict in question. Only in individual psychotherapy of children are the guidelines of psychotherapeutic conduct handled somewhat more loosely. In the play session with a child the psychotherapist may, by tentatively taking on roles of various adults, convey to the child what those adults are or might be like in the child's life. Even then, the role the therapist takes can be viewed as attempts at interpretations. "Is he or she like that?" is the therapist's implied question, and ultimately the child itself must decide whether the person represented is like that or not, and whether he wants him to be like that or not. At any rate, even in classical group therapy the group leader is not acting as a teacher, a model, or a helper in the patients' daily lives. The only thing he cannot help showing is how he intervenes in the group and how he guides its discourse. Ordinarily his interventions are not a matter for group discussion, however, unless he makes a mistake. If he does not listen properly or correctly or if a personal opinion on politics or social values slips from his lips, the group may want to take it up.

The group leader's behavior in the group is noticed by group members the same way a patient in individual therapy observes how the therapist encounters him and relates to his interests, feelings, and conflicts. Yet the patient cannot tell at first; he is too absorbed in dealing with his present life situation and his past. Only toward the end of psychotherapy does he manage to anticipate the psychotherapist's interventions more often. He has identified with the therapist and the therapist's ways of handling problems; the patient can handle them himself now. If a patient does not arbitrarily try to outguess the therapist, and if identification with the therapist eventually happens spontaneously and without design, termination of psychotherapy may soon be indicated. If the patient tries to do that early in the treatment, it often amounts to *acting out*. A patient may be trying to avoid his fears and conflicts by overtly adopting the therapist's interpretations or by testing his own courage in situations, in which according to the therapist, he is actually quite afraid. The patient is attempting to impress the therapist and to prove him wrong by his deeds.

All this happens in group therapy too. Group members rarely try to intervene in the beginning of treatment in the same way as the group leader. When they do so, they usually fail, and the group leader or group members tend to correct them. Yet, if the group anticipates correctly the leader's interventions without purposefully trying to, the end of group treatment may be near. Group members have then identified with the group leader and his ways of dealing with them. They can now act as they assume their group leader would.

One of the disadvantages of group therapy is the need to share the group leader's attention with other group members. There is neither enough time nor enough opportunity to talk about oneself. The group as a whole sets the pace. This is compensated, however, by an advantage briefly indicated before: a patient can observe how other patients behave or would like to behave in similar situations and conflicts. Group members may not only display counter-

transference behavior toward each other and respond whichever way they feel; they may also contribute to the group
their impressions and experiences, their conflicts, and their
attempts at resolution. They may teach each other or they
may learn from one another. Ordinarily they will derive from
other group members more diversified examples of people
achieving goals and gratifying interests than a patient might
ever muster in individual therapy. Fearsome and sorrowful
situations, which an individual patient wants to avoid at first
or to approach only with great hesitation in his memories
and thoughts, are being presented quite abruptly by other
members in group therapy. Before he has time to maneuver
a defense, the discussion is already rolling. He is learning
about possibilities of coping with events that he may never
have thought of himself.

MODELS FOR FAMILY THERAPY

From both fields of experience, child therapy and group
therapy, the idea emerged among some therapists to try a
special group: the family. Yet, historically speaking, the
pioneers of family therapy were neither child therapists nor
ordinary group therapists but those clinicians who had been
treating juvenile and adult patients with infantile personality
structures, namely, psychotic patients, particularly schizophrenics.

Psychoses had been termed narcissistic neuroses by
Freud (1916–1917); he had questioned whether they could be
treated by psychoanalysis. Such patients were extremely
ambivalent toward people important in their lives and had
therefore regressed psychologically to a preambivalent, nonperson state of mind and were unable to enter into a
transference bond with the psychotherapist that was spontaneous and stable enough to be utilized therapeutically.

Psychotherapists could not prevent the psychotic patient from feeling mortally jilted when they tried to trace his erratic transference responses—of overwhelming affection, of terror, of unbearable hatred, or of utter aloofness and frigidity—to their origins in the patient's reality and past. "If you are not available to me in a completely different way, much more often, with all your might and love, if you don't want to be my total protector, my friend, and my teacher, I will have nothing to do with you." That's what the psychotic patient seemed to be saying when the psychotherapist tried to act psychoanalytically or classically.

Since this demand of psychotic patients implies permanence—they want such a protector, friend, and teacher forever—there are limits to what any psychotherapist can do for them. He could offer these patients lifelong friendship only by accepting a few such patients and spending the rest of his working time with others who would not need him as protector and teacher but could help themselves after a while; or he could spend all his working time with psychotic patients, still not too many, and stick it out with them forever.

A third possibility was to recruit such a protector and friend for the patient: a friend who would take guidance from the therapist or stay with the patient of his own accord and, depending on the severity of his psychotic regression, treat him like an infant, a child, or a youth, even though he had long reached adulthood. But where can one get such a friend for the patient? And what would that friend get in return if he was not already the patient's friend? If the psychotic patient was married, the spouse was one such potential friend, to be sure. If he was not married, the more likely case, one could search for such a friend in the patient's family of origin. Who but the parents or a sibling of the patient—or, perhaps, an uncle, an aunt, a grandparent, or a cousin—would be more qualified? As it turned out, even in the patient's family a friend was hard to come by. In some families this was the last thing family members wanted to be. They had brought him to the mental hospital precisely because the patient was intolerable at home. They wanted to be rid of him. He was a pest.

Theories of the genesis of psychotic illness differ widely. Freud is said to have opposed the views of classical psychiatry (e.g., Kraepelin 1883) and its belief in organic and constitutional causes (which, however, had never been identified). The environment and the individual's responses play a major part, and psychological illness derives from environmental disruptions. Yet Freud allowed for a physiological component too. Some persons are born with such a weak constitution that even the slight hardships and frustrations of an average environment overtax them and make them ill. Other people are so robust that even grave environmental disturbances, such as the loss of parents or an early switch to foster parents, cannot permanently harm them (Freud 1916–1917).

This view is so sensible that few have tried to refute it. What should be said, though, is that in practice the influence of psychological disposition is not easy to appraise. It can be done only indirectly, only by an elimination procedure (Toman 1968, 1978b). When in an exploration of psychopathological development no environmental disruptions or damages can be found, when no traumatic events, no losses of family members or of other important persons have occurred, the likelihood increases that the person concerned may have an organic handicap. However, when such traumatic events have occurred, they could be connected to the psychopathology the person has developed. The kind of connection is another question.

Psychotherapeutic procedures tend to depend on an a priori decision. Whenever there is a constitutional or congenital deficiency, the person may require supportive psychotherapy, in which the therapist may act as a guardian, teacher, and model or may recruit such a guardian for the patient. When there have been environmental disruptions, there is hope that their adverse effects can be alleviated or healed by classical psychotherapy.

This plausible concept of two components notwithstanding—psychological constitution and environmental influences—one group of psychotherapists dealing with psychotic patients claimed that psychopathology is the result of environmental influences only, or, to be precise, of disturbed communications between the members of a person's family of origin. Since parents determine and shape those communications to a greater extent than their children do, parents are, according to this theory, more or less at fault when their children become mentally ill (e.g., Bateson et al. 1956, Laing et al. 1966, Watzlawick et al. 1967). Communication therapists conclude that parents and patients must learn to talk differently to each other (see also page 11 above) and to avoid contradictory or ambiguous communications. The parents and patient need more practice in constructive verbal and nonverbal communication.

What seems to have been overlooked is the possibility of a child's congenital psychological weakness. A child may be unable to wait; he may need gratification of all his needs more promptly and urgently than other children. Because of his extreme sensitivity both to external stimulation and to inner needs, he often is in or near panic and can help himself only by switching to gratifications that require no waiting. The child turns to experiences that he can control and even expand on all by himself. He does not want to heed other persons and their wishes and does not want to identify with them even though he is, in fact, dependent on them. On account of the child's impatience, his low tolerance for frustration, and his great ambivalence toward the persons around him, whom he hates vehemently if they don't tend immediately to his needs, interactions and communications between the child and his caretakers and nurturers are particularly difficult. Parents often complain early in the child's life that he does not smile, at least not when one would expect him to, that he balks and cramps in protest to many or any of the parents' touches, or accepts them with complete indifference and apathy. Communication therapists seem to imply that it is nevertheless the task of parents to engage in communication with such children the way other parents do with their ordinary offspring.

Whichever causation of psychoses psychotherapists believe in, many of them have apparently been trying to treat psychoses in similar ways. They were attempting to recruit a natural guardian and friend for the patient, if possible from his or her own family. There they met with various surprises. It turned out that changes in the patient would precipitate changes among other family members. As the pathology of the *identified patient* receded, psychological troubles of another family member or even of the family as a whole increased. The patient appeared to have fulfilled an important function in the family. One family member liked the patient's dependence; another family member hated him for the excessive care and consideration he commanded or for the turmoil he created in the family. A conflict between two family members' views of the patient turned out to be a conflict between those family members themselves; the patient was merely their unconscious pretense (Ackerman 1958, Auerbach 1959, Bateson et al. 1956, Bell and Vogel 1960, Bowen 1959, Jackson 1960).

In general, families with psychotic patients were different from families without such patients. In families with a psychotic member, other family members, too, were in need of emotional support and depended on each other. At least one other person in the family typically had difficulty differentiating himself in the family and difficulty becoming his own person. Not infrequently, that other infantile personality was a parent. Moreover, the parents often had conflicts with each other, but they rarely talked about them. They had expectations vis-à-vis their children and each other that had already developed in their families of origin and had not been quite realistic even then. Unfulfilled sexual wishes toward the spouse may not have escaped the children's notice. Parents often project onto their children some of the expectations and demands imposed on them by their parents. Children become confused about these projections, particularly when the parents disagree between themselves about their expectations. Some parents had not really separated themselves from their own parents. If the other parent did not compensate for this by exceptional independence from his own family of origin or from both families, the parents of the mother and those of the father may have found themselves implicated in the struggle for the welfare of the family and the health of the children (Ackerman 1958, Bowen 1959, Fairbairn 1952, Guntrip 1969, Ruesch and Bateson 1951, Winnicott 1965).

These complicated relationships have been observed in psychotherapy of psychotic patients and their families, but also in therapies of families in which not a single family member showed any clear evidence of psychopathology. Family therapists began to view the family as a system of relationships: no change can occur without concurrent changes somewhere else in the system. Even the family's resistance to change was a characteristic of that system. The existing network of relationships tended to preserve itself. If it changed, the system as a whole was to be maintained.

The family must not break up, it seemed. When a family member leaves, other members must take over his functions. When a new person is added either for the first time or returning after a prolonged absence, most or all family members are usually affected. Their roles and tasks change in part and have to be retuned. When a family member befriends a person outside the family or falls in love, the entire family is affected. A fight to keep the member in the family or to repel the foreigner may ensue. Family members may have to hide their more important extrafamilial relationships from the family in order not to jeopardize those relationships.

In trying to understand such family-system characteristics, some family therapists consulted with system theorists. What Parsons had attempted to describe in macro- and family-sociological terms (Parsons 1951, Parsons and Bales 1955), Grinker (1956) and his team of authors tried to apply to human behavior in general, Toman (1959a, b, 1961) to the large variety of family contexts, Gray (1969) and colleagues to psychopathological phenomena (Ackerman 1958, Bateson et al. 1956, Bertalanffy 1968, Bowen 1959, 1960, 1965, 1978, Lidz et al. 1965, Midelfort 1957, Wynne et al. 1960). These therapists also included in their considerations the effects of a family therapist's contact with the family.

They all had little doubt about the need for classical psychotherapy. As in individual and group therapy, the family therapist could hope to be therapeutically effective only by exercising self-restraint and social abstinence, by avoiding friendships with individual family members or the family as a whole, and by restricting his contacts with the family to therapy sessions. The family therapist would not reveal his personal life in any way. He might express notions, though, of a better or a more sincere family life. In this respect he would occasionally be acting as a teacher or model. He would guide and support the family in their attempts to recognize better the wishes and interests of family members and to find more congenial conflict resolutions than they had reached so far. Yet he would not reveal anything substantial about his own family life nor introduce any of his own family members to them.

Styles of Treatment

The personality of a psychotherapist tends to show more in family therapy than it does in individual psychotherapy because of the complex and highly emotional issues that surface in treatment. The family therapist exposes himself more distinctly, more variedly, and, in the eyes of different family members, often more ambiguously than an individual therapist. He may talk loudly or softly, may wait a long time to get a word in, or interrupt the family discourse soon and often. The therapist may be talkative or quiet or ingratiating or reserved, in his comments, questions, and interpretations regarding the motives, interests, and conflicts that he thinks he can recognize in family members. It depends not only on what he hears and sees, but also on his own idiosyncrasies.

Family therapy is more complex than individual therapy; the therapist's challenge is greater. The family therapist is called upon to make every effort possible to meet the challenge the complex therapy presents. He is lucky when the family lets him conduct classical psychotherapy. He must prevail in the family and must preserve a measure of control so that at any time during the session he can be available for each family member. Whether he likes it or not, more than in individual therapy he is the director of the process. He allows people to speak or denies them permission; he may stop them when need be. He insists on some of his commentaries and interpretations and may explicitly take others back. He offers his opinion of what happened in the session and chooses the times to repeat interpretations or to summarize.

It is all-important in this respect that the family therapist should not be suffering from any personal or family problems of his own. He must not misperceive the course of the discussion and interactions among family members through his own transferences and projections onto the family in treatment. Fulfilling needs such as being a great therapist, a more charming person, a better father, or sweeter mother than the parents in the family before him, or satisfying cravings for tender or intimate contacts with a member of that family are prohibited. He must remain an objective, sympathetic, yet neutral observer. He must recognize what goes on under the surface and where the treatment is going in both the short and long term. That helps him convey to family members the calm and self-confidence that they need in order to venture at all into a family talk with a stranger present. Basically the therapist ought to be able to justify whatever he says and does, even if no one ever takes him up on it.

Family therapy may be orchestrated in various forms, ranging from an invitation to all family members at the beginning of treatment to an initial contact with only one family member who may gradually pull in others. Attendance by all family members, or at least by all those who consented to come, may be enforced strictly or loosely or not at all. Family therapy may involve only a part of the family—occasionally just a single member. On the other hand, it may include members of the extended family: the grandparents, an uncle, an old family friend, or even a neighbor.

Some family therapists, after a while, are inclined to keep only the parents in treatment. The children may stay home, especially when the parents are discussing their very personal problems. Other family therapists do not agree, claiming that parents cannot really hide personal problems from their children. Although family therapy sometimes focuses on the relationship between one parent and only one of the children, it neither restricts interactions with other family members nor discourages discussions about them. They are merely not requested to appear before the therapist.

Some family therapists have been treating several families—or at least several couples of parents—at once. This arrangement could be called group therapy for parental couples (Framo 1973, Laqueur 1973). In certain instances, however, the family therapist may not allow the couples much interaction (Bowen 1971). Those couples that are not engaged in talking to the family therapist at any given moment are watching and listening until it is their turn.

Many family therapists prefer to work in pairs, usually a man and a woman. If they are well suited to each other, they find it easier to observe the family. Two hear and see more than one, and while one is talking, the other can more readily look around. They can also keep better tabs on the family members' individual relationship toward each therapist. The family is in effect being offered both a father and a mother figure, and they can place their transferences and projections with greater discrimination on two therapists than they can on one. This tends to hold true even when the therapists are two men or two women.

Additional references on these variations are Friedmann (1965), Gerlicher and colleagues (1977), Meistermann-Seeger (1976), Minuchin (1974), Pakesch (1973), Richter (1970), Satir (1967), and Stierlin (1975). Bloch (1973), Boszormenyi-Nagy and Framo (1965), Glick and Haley (1971), Richter and colleagues (1976), and Toman (1977) offer overviews.

3

FAMILY CONSTELLATIONS AND CONFIGURATIONS

In order to understand family life and its possible disturbances in a particular family, we need to survey the ordinary or average family and its development. In any given family current family life as well as family life in the past is of interest. The way the parents grew up in their families has provided them with ideas about family life and has guided them in their own efforts to form a partnership and raise a family. Even when young parents want to do the opposite of what they saw their own parents do, the family life of the previous generation has an influence on them. Later on we shall concern ourselves with whether it is at all possible in essential matters to do the opposite of what one has perceived and experienced.

In spite of the many efforts of educators, politicians, scientists, and the mass media to change and facilitate family life, particularly for women, life in the average family has not changed very much in the last fifty or sixty years—at least for both urban and town life in industrial nations. Even in villages, family life is looking more and more like family life in the cities and towns. The family clan, wherein grandparents, parents, and children, aunts, uncles, and their children are living together or nearby, is now disappearing even in rural areas. The men have to go to town and city for work. Geographic mobility has increased and the number of children has declined. Often sizable distances separate the family clan from each other. Grandparents and their siblings—that is, the uncles and aunts of the parents—are often hard to get to. Visits require explicit invitations and sometimes long journeys.

FAMILY DATA

The average family has two to three children—in the cities often just one or two. At the time of marriage the father usually is between 25 and 28 years old (the mean is 27 years), the mother between 22 and 25 (the mean being 24 years). On the average, the wife is about three years younger than the husband. At different historical periods and in different social strata these mean ages vary, but the average age difference between husband and wife has remained about three years. In only 10 percent of all marriages with children the husband is ten or more years older than his wife. In only 15 percent of all marriages is the wife one or more years older than the husband.

In many instances, the first child arrives one to two years after the wedding, the second child three to four years later. With three or more children, the age distances between them tend to be a bit smaller. Nine out of ten families stay intact until their children (or their middle one) have reached age 15 or 16. Both parents are physically present. One in ten families, however, has suffered the loss of a parent and/or a sibling during that time, and one in twenty families, has experienced the loss of a parent during one of their children's first six years of life. This includes families in which one parent, usually the father (i.e., five times more often than the mother) has never lived in the family.

In many families, the father works outside the home and the mother takes care of the house and looks after the children even though she may have worked prior to marriage. Some mothers keep working at least part time through early motherhood. They either hire somebody to take care of the children while they are out, or an institution helps them (such as day-care centers, nursery schools, kindergartens, and eventually school). In only a few families does the mother work full time and the father takes care of the house and children. Single parents are, of course, another story.

The arrival of more children often requires the parents to move to a larger home. On the average, families change homes once or twice. In three out of four families a child comes down with an average of three illnesses; in one of four families, it increases to four or more illnesses. Among half of all families one of these illnesses (or accidents) necessitates hospitalization, which in most cases lasts less than four weeks (Toman 1974, Toman and Preiser 1973).

FOUNDING A FAMILY

Even today, many couples decide but once in their lives to stay together and establish a common household. However, divorces have steadily increased through the last decades and more people than ever before are married for the second time. Couples living together without being married have also increased. Those who eventually marry seem to take longer than ever to do so. More often, unmarried couples separate and form new partnerships.

Even if a couple moves in together for the first time, this event is not quite as unique and new to them, psychologically speaking, as it appears. Usually both partners have known and considered other candidates for such a partnership; they have had small doses of living together when they went out to dine, when they spent evenings, nights, weekends, or vacations together. People have had those concrete experiences to varying degrees and duration, but with all of them something was left to their imagination—and imagine they did, or at least try to.

Going-to-be spouses have another source of information: They know other couples among their acquaintances and friends who are married and may even have children; still other couples are expressing such intentions. From their observations of such couples, new partners can develop their own wishes and designs and exchange their views about them.

Last but not least, all going-to-be spouses have known life in their families of origin. They know from their parents what love and marriage is like. They participated in their wedded life long before they began to consciously realize what it was all about. The major depth psychologists (e.g., Adler, Freud, Jung, Schultz-Hencke, Sullivan) all assume that a person's most elementary and enduring experiences are those he had with his parents and siblings. The example of his parents as well as the experience of relating to siblings early on as he sees the parents relate to each other and to the children is an important body of knowledge to draw from in a person's choice of friends in kindergarten, in school, at work, and ultimately even in the choice of a partner for love and life. Considering all these varieties of relevant experience, new partners are not really tumbling into the unknown when they decide to join forces for the first time in their lives (Toman 1961, 1965, 1968, 1978b).

FAMILY CONSTELLATIONS

People's experiences in their families of origin can be distinguished from each other by a comparatively small number of permanent and objective characteristics. Among them are the geographic, ethnic, religious, and economic characteristics. Whether a family has been living in the country or in a town or city, in the mountains or at the sea, whether it belongs to the majority or a minority of the population, whether it speaks the national language or a foreign one, whether its members differ greatly or not at all from the majority in height, in build, in skin and hair color, in dress, etc.—all these are such enduring characteristics and are often of no small significance for those concerned. Economic and cultural dimensions, such as the parents' assets and income, living conditions, neighborhood, opportunities for education and travel, access to cultural and sports activities, etc., may all vary greatly from family to family.

Modern democracies are attempting to level those differences, at least for the next generation. Accordingly, children should have equal opportunities for individual growth when they start. If they eventually develop differently and if the differences increase with time, these discrepancies may be due to the children's unequal native talents or to their unequal motivation and effort. When families are similar to each other with respect to such permanent and objective characteristics, they may still differ considerably in other ways: They may have few or many children, and the children may be few or many years apart in age; they may be boys, girls, or both and may be many years younger than their parents or relatively close in age. The parents themselves may have come from large or small families. In short, the composition of families varies widely even if only number, gender, and age distribution are considered.

When both parents are living in the family and average conditions prevail, different compositions or configurations of children in the family or different positions within a given configuration of children may still have very different psychological effects.

A family of two children only may consist of two boys, two girls, a boy and a girl or a girl and a boy. The sibling positions that a child can have in a two-child family are:

older brother of brother	b(b)
younger brother of brother	(b)b
older brother of sister	b(s)
younger brother of sister	(s)b
older sister of sister	s(s)
younger sister of sister	(s)s
older sister of brother	s(b)
younger sister of brother	(b)s

These eight sibling positions are contained in all more complicated sibling positions. The older brother of a sister and brother, b(sb), for example, is holding two sibling positions in his family: that of an older brother of sister and that of an older brother of brother. The middle sister of two brothers (b)s(b), is both a younger sister of brother and an older sister of brother.

The eight sibling positions outlined can hence be called the basic or main types of sibling position. All other sibling positions are composed of them. Only the *single child* is a special case. He, or she, has no sibling position. His social relationships within the family are restricted to his parents and to his observations of them, whereas children with siblings also have relationships with those siblings and may imitate in their sibling relationships their own interactions with their parents, and even what they see their parents doing to each other.

Relationships within Basic Types
of Child Configurations

In a family of two boys, the older one has been a single child for some three to four years, on the average, before his brother arrives. After registering initial protests against the newcomer, he typically grows into a role of responsibility and leadership; he has to protect his little brother. The younger brother, on the other hand, knows no other life than that with a big brother and develops feelings of dependency and trust, and eventually of competitiveness and opposition. The older brother understands his parents, and later on his teachers, better than the younger brother does. The younger brother responds more strongly and more impulsively to social stimuli that emanate from his brother, from siblings in general, and from other children on playgrounds and in school.

In a family of two girls the older one is again frequently three to four years older than her sister. She, too, has been a single child and the sole focus of her parents' attention before they began to insist that she share them with this helpless and demanding newcomer. She, too, takes on responsibility and the task of leadership. Whatever the younger sister may do, the big sister will have to protect her and come to her rescue. She admires the older sister, has practically never been alone, and cannot very well imagine life without her. She can compete with her, though, and behave spitefully toward her. The older sister identifies more with her parents and with persons in positions of authority; the younger one is more likely to oppose or compete with them. The younger sister tends to respond more impetuously and dependently to siblings and to other children than does an older sister.

Children in both child configurations, two boys as well as two girls, get accustomed to life with a peer of the same sex only. They lack experience with peers of the opposite sex except when they watch how their parents behave. However, they cannot very well practice with their sibling what they observe between their parents. In their relations with the opposite-sex parent there is more than the ordinary competition. In a family of two sons, three males are vying for mother's love; in a family of two daughters, three females are competing for father's favors. In both families both children can primarily identify themselves only with the same-sex parent, the boys with the father, the girls with the mother.

In a family with a son first and a daughter next, after an average of three or four years as a single child, the boy is learning to care for his little sister, to guide and protect her even if at first he resents the responsibility and does not like her. His little sister grows up with the feeling that she can rely on her brother, that she may do what she wants and he will attend to her and help her, but also that in certain matters she will have to knuckle under and follow suit. The two children are in no great competitive struggle with each other. Each child can identify with a different parent; the boy with the father, the girl with the mother. Both children can play and practice together, imitating what they see their parents do to each other; each of them, moreover, can interact with the opposite-sex parent and thereby temporarily substitute for the same-sex parent.

In a family with a daughter first and a son second, the girl is learning how to treat her little brother maternally. After some initial resistance she usually has no trouble accepting the role her parents assigned to her. Her occasional envy of the boy who gets so much parental attention and affection can be dispelled more easily than that of other, older siblings. A reminder that so far it is she who has had the parents all to herself (for three or four years, under average circumstances) tends to readily pacify her. The boy, however, has had a big sister as long as he can remember. She has always helped and protected him, he feels, and done things for him that he could not or would not do for himself. Since he is the first boy in the family, the parents tend to grant him more privileges than other younger siblings; he gets away with everything. They pamper him, big sister sometimes complains. Even so, she and her brother feel less competitive about each other than do two brothers or two sisters. They can identify with different parents (she with mother and he with father). In relation to the opposite-sex parent each of the children can playfully take the position of the same-sex parent and temporarily substitute for him or her. Finally, both children can model their relationship to each other on that of their parents.

In both configurations, older brother and younger sister as well as older sister and younger brother, the children are getting used to life with a peer of the opposite sex. What they do not learn so well is how to get along or live with a peer of the same sex (Toman 1961, 1974, 1976).

More Complex Child Configurations

When there are more than two children in a family, conditions and relationships become more complicated. The older brother of two or three sisters resembles the older brother of one sister in his social expectations and preferences: For each of his sisters he is an older brother. The two or three sisters, however, compete with each other in a certain way for the brother's attention. They also have a relationship to build among themselves. In contrast with their brother they have more than one type of sibling relationship.

When an older brother has four or even more younger sisters and no brothers, things are still more complicated. The sisters' relationships among each other weigh more heavily in subjective meaning than does their relationship with the brother. In this instance the brother becomes somewhat isolated. The scramble for his attention and interest may be so intense on the other hand, that not much is left for each of the girls. Another possibility: one or two sisters form a close relationship with him, the remaining ones cling to each other.

The same holds true for the youngest brother of several sisters as well as for the oldest or the youngest sister of several brothers. They all are likely to be reinforced in their respective sibling roles by two or even three siblings of the other sex, but the struggle for the unique sibling intensifies with the number of siblings of the other sex. With three or more other-sex siblings, subgroups may form among the children.

Middle siblings always have at least two different types of sibling relationships. The middle brother of two sisters is both the younger and the older brother of a sister. Not infrequently he can assume both roles equally well. Due to special circumstances such as very discrepant age differences from his two siblings or parental preference, one role may be more pronounced than the other. If a middle brother has several older and several younger sisters, subgroups may form. Then he may either become the younger brother of an older sister or the older brother of a younger sister. The greater the number of sisters, the more unique and precious he may be in the eyes of the parents. A special and envied position among the children may result, in some instances even his isolation. This is also true for a middle sister of brothers only. She, too, will usually be treasured and cared for more than the other children. She is the rare sex in the family. Nothing must happen to her.

The middle sibling who has both an older and a younger sister and an older and a younger brother holds four types of sibling roles; nothing is left out. As a result, he is likely to be in the least conspicuous position among his siblings. One of them is the oldest girl, one the youngest girl; one the oldest boy, one the youngest boy. The middle sibling is neither. He (or she) tends to experience himself/herself as less important than any of his brothers and sisters and does not know how to reverse the situation. More than any of his siblings he strives to find a place and role outside his family and their expectations.

In configurations consisting of many children there are more middle siblings than in small child configurations. Middle siblings grow up in less pronounced positions and roles than do the oldest and the youngest. There are exceptions to this when subgroups form among siblings. A middle sibling may become the youngest or the oldest of a subgroup. This more defined position may, at least, imbue him or her with some of the characteristics of that position.

About 1 percent of all children are twins. In spite of the fact that there is no age difference between them to speak of, they do in part resemble ordinary siblings: One of them assumes the role of the older or is appointed to it; the other, that of the younger. If they have other siblings, twins assume the characteristics that a single child would have in their position. If they have younger siblings, both of them act like oldest siblings themselves. If all their siblings are older, both of them appear and behave like youngest siblings.

Exceptionally small age differences tie siblings very closely to each other, whereas unusually large age differences (six or more years) tend to make quasi-singletons of two siblings. When in a sibling configuration there is a large age distance between adjacent sibling groups, the siblings may divide into subgroups.

Unusual physical or mental characteristics may modulate a child's position in a sibling configuration and thus affect the entire lot. Great physical strength or extraordinary intelligence may enable a middle or even a youngest sibling to assume the interests and tasks of an oldest sibling as the children all grow older. He advances in his age rank, so to speak. Under ordinary circumstances higher age-rank automatically implies a lead in intelligence, experience, and power. Inversely, a physically weak, sickly, or mentally retarded oldest child may fall behind his siblings and become dependent on them before long. His age rank recedes as the children grow older.

Physical resemblances or talents similar to parents or certain relatives may create an unusual family interest in a particular child—or sometimes an aversion. A mother may feel ambivalent toward one of her children because he looks and acts like her father whom she had hated. A father may spoil one of his daughters because she looks like his favorite sister or a former girlfriend.

Relationships between Marriage Partners

A couple planning children at first do not know when and at what intervals they are going to have them nor how many there will be, but both spouses begin the adventure with certain hopes and expectations.

As we have observed, those hopes and expectations derive from their own experiences in their families of origin. It has been demonstrated (Toman 1961, 1965, especially third edition 1976) that a person, in shaping new long-term social relationships, leans on his or her experiences in the family of origin. One tends to be comparatively happier and more successful in permanent relationships, the closer they resemble earlier relationships, particularly those of the original family. I have called this imprecise, but heuristically useful statement the *duplication theorem* (Toman 1961, 1965, 1971).

This implies for spouses, that, other things being equal, they get along better with each other, the more their partner resembles a sibling of theirs. An older brother of a sister, for example, would match well with a younger sister of a brother: b(s)/(b)s. In this symbolic expression the slash means partnership or friendship. Likewise, a younger brother of a sister would fare well with an older sister of a brother: (s)b/s(b). The partners of both couples, in their families of origin, have been used to life with a peer of the opposite sex. What is more, they have different age ranks: one partner has been an older sibling, the other, a younger. So in both couples the partners have *complementary sibling roles*.

On the other hand, the more closely marriage partners resemble each other, the easier it ordinarily is for them to empathize with each other but the harder to live together. The oldest brother of a brother and the oldest sister of a sister [b(b)/s(s)], for example, have both learned to assume leadership and responsibility, but their partners will not let them; each wants to be the leader. Moreover, in their original sibling configuration neither has been used to life with a peer of the opposite sex. We could say that by virtue of their sibling roles these partners have an *age-rank as well as a sex conflict*. The same would hold for a younger brother of a brother married to a younger sister of a sister [symbolically, (b)b/(s)s]. Both of them seek leadership from the other and can't get it, and both of them have been used to life only with peers of the same sex, not with the opposite sex. They, too, have both an age-rank and a sex conflict of sibling roles.

Among partners coming from sibling configurations of two children only, there are other possible matches (sixteen in all). The older brother of a sister can choose an older or a younger sister of a brother or of a sister, the younger brother of a sister likewise—and the same holds for the older brother of a brother and the younger brother of a brother. However, the complementary matches described—b(s)/(b)s and (s)b/s(b)—and the noncomplementary matches burdened by age-rank and sex conflicts of sibling roles—b(b)/s(s) and (b)b/(s)s—are the most and the least favorable, respectively.

This interpretation of sibling-role combinations has been confirmed by hard empirical data. Assuming that happy and successful marriages ought to last, divorces would obviously indicate less happy and less successful marriages. In a sample of 2,300 families with children, 5 percent of the parents were divorced. This corresponded well with the divorce rate in the population. Among those couples, however, whose sibling roles were complementary there was not a single divorce case. Among those couples whose sibling roles showed both an age-rank and a sex conflict, 16 percent had been divorced (Toman 1971, 1974, 1976, Toman and Preiser 1973). Among couples whose both partners had been single children, that is, had grown up with no sibling experience at all, 9 percent had been divorced.

From these and other findings reported in addition to Toman 1974, 1976, it could be established that complementarity or partial complementarity of sibling roles of marriage partners corresponds with a stronger wish for children, statistically speaking—that is, a significantly larger number of children that they generated (about half a child more than the average) corresponds with an easier life together as well as with the children. Children of parents with complementary sibling roles consulted psychological guidance centers less frequently than would be expected by chance and less frequently than children of parents whose sibling roles showed age-rank and sex conflicts or who had (both) been single children. When children of parents with complementary sibling roles did consult psychological guidance centers, their complaints tended to be minor compared with children of parents with age-rank and sex conflicts of sibling roles.

Between the extremes of complementarity of spouses' sibling roles—for example, b(s)/(b)s or b(ss)/(bbb)s or (s)b/s(bb)—and age-rank and sex conflict in sibling roles—(b)b/(s)s or (bb)b/(sss)s—there are intermediate forms. One has already been mentioned: partial complementarity.

One may speak of *partial complementarity* of sibling roles when marriage partners have come from larger sibling configurations with several sibling relationships, among which there is at least one that is complementary to at least one of the partner's. For example, the older brother of a brother and a sister, b(bs), and the middle sister of two brothers, (b)s(b), both have one complementary relationship: he is the older brother of a sister, she the younger sister of a brother. They have other sibling relationships that do not fit their partnership: he is also the older brother of a brother, she the older sister of a brother. It is reasonable to assume, though, that partners will draw on their experiences with those sibling relationships that fit their partner and close off the others or use them only outside their partnership, say in an additional friendship.

Spouses may have age-rank conflicts of sibling roles but no sex conflicts—for instance, b(s)/s(b) or sex conflicts without age-rank conflicts, b(b)/(s)s. We are dealing with moderate sibling-role conflict. If one partner has no sibling role conflict whereas the other does—e.g., b(s)/(s)s—their sibling role conflict would be considered mild. We may suppose that the partner who by his sibling experience has been better prepared for marriage, like the husband in our example, will tend to lead the way and show his spouse how to live together with a peer of the opposite sex.

If both partners have an age-rank conflict and one of them a sex conflict too, the sibling role conflict would be more severe. The younger brother of a brother and the younger sister of a brother [(b)b/(b)s] is an example, Compared with a combined age-rank and sex conflict of both partners, however, this is a little better, since the wife has had a heterosexual sibling. She knows how to live with a brother and may be able to translate that experience to her relationship with her husband (see Toman 1974, especially p. 191 ff., and Toman 1976, p. 198 ff.).

Spouses who suffer both an age-rank and a sex conflict

with respect to their sibling roles are not doomed. I have pointed out that in one study 16 percent of such marriage partners with children had been divorced. Yet this means that 84 percent of these marriage partners stayed together and could apparently tolerate each other well enough. Clinical-psychological and psychotherapeutic experience with such spouses suggests, however, that they arrange their partnership differently than do couples with complementary sibling roles. Spouses with age-rank and sex conflicts are less emotionally close with each other, even though they have intimate relations and children. They need same-sex friendships more than other couples (such as one finds in men's and women's clubs, sports, drinking, or gambling, on one hand, and social welfare activities on the other). They have to give each other more leeway for such purposes than other couples. If they do, their marriage tends to be stronger.

One more word about single children as spouses. They actually search for parent-like persons for partners. Hence, they get along better with mates who are oldest siblings than they do with others. Frequently they prefer partners of greater than average age distance from themselves. When they are older than their respective partners, single children can also get along with partners who are middle or youngest siblings.

The prognosis is relatively poor when two single children marry each other. However, their compatibility may be better or worse depending on whether the sibling roles of their respective same-sex parents are complementary or not. Through identification with the same-sex parent single children can adopt that parent's sibling role, at least in part.

Relationships between Parents and Children

All parents are more or less surprised by life with their first-born child. If they had younger siblings in their families of origin, they might remember their births, but that memory is vague. Their early sufferings at the hands of that newcomer were usually more memorable than their first good experiences, but as time passed, things tended to improve. When the parents had no younger siblings, they do not have even these vague memories to draw on. All parents, however, have heard about newborns and have seen what life with them is like among their relatives and friends, in the neighborhood, in books and magazines, on television, and in parent-training courses, and so on, and the great majority of all going-to-be parents can recruit some relatives and friends who have had and raised children themselves and who are willing to offer them their counsel and help. Such guidance is usually welcome, particularly during the first days and weeks of the newborn child. Yet before long the young parents, above all the young mother, know more about the child and his needs than all the other people around them, even the most welcome counselors and helpers. At any rate, many parents get used to their first child comparatively quickly, and the children that follow, as a rule, give them no great trouble.

The parents' relationships to their children are not so much determined by those first weeks of their children's lives, but by that which endures as they live together from day to day and year to year. It is not the little events and accidents of the first contacts and interactions with the child that matter but rather the attitudes and' sentiments of the parents toward each other and toward the child; attitudes and sentiments that existed even before the child was born and that persist long after birth. In fact, these enduring ways of thinking and feeling determine some of the little events and accidents that mark the parents' early contacts and interactions with the child, rather than vice versa.

If happily married spouses have wished for a child and eventually get one, they can almost do no wrong. If spouses are in conflict with one another, however, or if one or both of them did not really want a child, but rather had it for their parents' sake or to keep up with the neighbors, perhaps to rescue their own faltering marriage, to tie their spouse to themselves or to punish him or her, it becomes hard for them to do anything right by the child. Even the most attentive treatment of the child can miss its wishes and needs. The parents do not even know what they themselves want from the child and for the child, or they do know, but their wishes contradict each other.

When it comes to the daily chores of child care over the months and years, the parents can more resourcefully utilize the experiences of their own childhood than they can during the child's first few days. These experiences include all that the parents remember about their early lives, all that their siblings have done to them and they to their siblings, and what they saw their parents do to them and their siblings. Many young parents, even those who had eventually rebelled against their own parents and run away from home, report that when they had children of their own they caught themselves doing the same things to their children that they remembered their parents doing to them. In difficult and new situations in which they could recall no parental paradigm, they even asked themselves: "What would my mother (or grandmother or father) have done in this situation?" With the help of such imaginative identification with their parents, they can often find practical solutions.

Parent–Child Relationships and the Sibling Positions of Parents and of Children

When in handling and caring for their children young parents utilize experiences they have had with their own siblings, those parents who were oldest or middle siblings have an edge on those who were youngest. In some fashion they have had to deal with the arrival and early care of their younger siblings. Parents who were youngest siblings themselves ordinarily have had no such opportunities. When there is an oldest or middle sibling among the two young parents, he or she will tend to lead the way in the care of their own child.

When both parents were oldest siblings, however, they will tend to compete for responsibility and leadership in handling their own children. Sometimes they divide the children among themselves and exert a kind of parallel influence on them. When one or both parents have come from monosexual sibling configurations (boys only or girls only), father usually takes on the sons and mother the daughters, provided they have both. In that way a "war of the sexes" mode may be instilled in the children—one that the children themselves would not engage in if left to their own resources.

When both parents were youngest siblings, they often feel helpless vis-à-vis their own child. They tend to lean on persons of authority and to have a strong need to be shown how to deal with children or to find someone who will do it in their stead. An older sibling of the parents or one of the mothers-in-law may sometimes be quite willing to step in. When their children have grown, these parents may surprise even themselves by the urgency with which they want to transform their own children into authority figures and confidants. Their oldest child may be called upon in this way quite early in his life. Often such parents are content to have only one child. Either way the child is usually overtaxed by those parental demands. He may be able to take on some of the manners of a senior for his parents but cannot keep it up, at least not outside the family.

In many families as parents and children live together— at least until the youngest child has turned 15 years of age and sometimes until it is much older—each parent forms a specific relationship to each of their children. Altogether there are $2n$ such relationships, if n is the number of children in the family. With two children there are four different parent–children relationships, with three children six, and so forth.

Since children also form relationships among themselves, this network is still more complicated. A family with two children entertains

$$\binom{4}{2} \text{ relationships, that is, } \frac{4 \cdot 3}{1 \cdot 2} = \text{ six relationships,}$$

a family with three children

$$\binom{5}{2} \text{ relationships, that is, } \frac{5 \cdot 4}{1 \cdot 2} = \text{ ten relationships,}$$

a family with four children fifteen, and so forth. How can one keep up with this as an observer? How can even a family member find his way through that maze?

Let us see what help we can derive from the duplication theorem (see p. 46). According to this theorem the parents' relationships to their children would be happier and more successful or at least would find growing up easier if the parents' situation in their original families was similar to that of their children. In that case parents and children would understand each other better and get along more readily than if their respective situations were different.

Since in an intact family each child develops a relationship with Father as well as with Mother, and since one of the parents is of the opposite sex from the child and one of the same sex, there obviously develop two different forms of parent–child relationship. Freud (1900, 1916–1917) and other depth psychologists such as Adler, Jung, Schultz-Hencke, or Sullivan have pointed them out.

The *relationship with the parent of the same sex*, after

occasional early confusion, develops into one of *identification*. A son takes after his father and adopts him as a model. The daughter becomes like her mother and imitates her. Such a relationship of identification is characterized by the fact that the two persons concerned resemble each other and can empathize with, understand, and even substitute for one another. When Father is absent, the son can take his part. When Mother is unavailable, the daughter may try to replace her in the family.

The relationship of the child with the *parent of the opposite sex* usually rests on their dissimilarity. Men and women are different in many respects, and their relationship is often geared to those differences. One person has and can do, what the other does not have and cannot do, but wants or needs. Divisions of interests such as professional versus household work, engineering versus art, politics versus religion, competitive sport versus entertainment, help with the children's homework in the sciences versus help in languages or literature are old stereotypes, but they are more widespread and relevant than one might think. The man is portrayed as strong, intelligent, if need be, aggressive, but also impatient and intolerant of pain; the woman, as beautiful and charming, more willing to give in, patient and bearing pain more gracefully. For ideological and practical reasons people want to get away from these stereotypes, and sometimes they succeed, but in the majority of parental couples and partnerships in love the sex roles tend to persist and are experienced as meaningful. Each love and marriage partner alone is incomplete, people believe, but together—complementing each other—the two can master life and the world.

In any case, among the couple's children the boy becomes the little man and the girl the little woman rather than vice versa. In identification with his father as well as by virtue of his own predilections and experiences, the boy develops a complementary relationship to his mother in which he can do things or wants to do things that she cannot do and hopes to get things from her that he cannot provide for himself. The girl acts likewise with Father. He is the big, strong man who protects her, and she has to be attentive, well-behaved, and beautiful. She admires him and wants to please him. Such are her intentions.

Identification of a child *with the same-sex parent* tends to be easier, the more father and son or mother and daughter resemble each other. Resemblance or similarity may be defined as the number of characteristics that apply in identical manner to both father and son or to mother and daughter. One of those characteristics is the sibling position or sibling role of the parent and child. The more similar the sibling position of a child is to that of the same-sex parent (other things being equal) the easier it is for the child to identify with the same-sex parent in his social behavior and attitudes, and the easier it is also for the parent to understand the child and identify with him. The less alike the sibling position of the child and that of the same-sex parent, the greater the identification conflict.

As for the child's *interaction with the opposite-sex parent*, interaction is easier, the greater the number of characteristics that are different or complementary, relatively speaking. They get along better and can live together more comfortably (other things being equal) the more complementary their sibling positions are.

What has been important in love and marriage relationships may thus be taken to matter in parent–child relationships. A daughter who is a younger sister of a brother, gets along particularly well with her father, and he with her, if Father has been an older brother of a sister himself. A son who has an older sister relates best to his mother, comparatively speaking, and she to him, if mother, too, has had a younger brother.

If, incidentally, that mother had an older brother as well, one may nevertheless assume that she will draw on her experiences with her younger brother in her relationships with her son. The sibling roles of mother and son reflect *partial* complementarity which, as we have seen, has favorable effects on a relationship. When that mother's husband, on the other hand, has been the older brother of a sister, mother is getting a replication of each of her two sibling relationships: Her husband is like her older brother, her son like her younger brother.

It should be noted that in such a case the son would have an identification conflict with his father. The sibling positions of father and son are dissimilar; on the basis of their experiences they have different ideas about, for example, how to deal with girls. Father thinks the son should act the leader and be responsible and protective; the son thinks that he can be carefree, self-centered, and relying on the girls' motherly instincts.

The considerations sketched in these paragraphs have been treated more elaborately elsewhere (e.g., Toman 1974, especially pp. 187 ff., Toman 1976, pp. 198 ff.). The professional, however, will probably spot and resolve these complexities in practice, provided that he or she does not crudely characterize a given family constellation, but analyze it from various aspects. What needs to be regarded is not only a person's sibling position, but also that of each parent, along with their relationship to one another and to their children.

We talked as if there were no question but that a child would always identify with the same-sex parent and interact with the opposite-sex parent. Yet secondary identifications will also develop with the opposite-sex parent, secondary interactions with the same-sex parent.

This may be the case when a family has only boys or only girls. Not infrequently one of the two or three boys will be urged to distinguish himself from his brothers: to become the artist rather than the sportsman or engineer—in other words more of a girl among the boys—and to identify more with Mother than with Father. In a family of two or more girls only, one will turn into the tomboy and become Father's apprentice in his shop or in his hobbies. Accordingly, she will identify with Father rather than with Mother.

Even when parents who have grown up in monosexual child configurations have both sons and daughters, they may aspire to interactive relationships with their same-sex children and, through their own inhibitions and shyness in their contacts with the opposite sex, may inspire their opposite-sex children to identify with them. People coming from monosexual sibling configurations often feel more esteem for friendships with persons of the same sex than for friendships with persons of the opposite sex or for love relationships in general. In the family described, comradeship and solidarity among men and women could dominate family life, perhaps even to the exclusion of any close relationships to family members of the other sex.

Parent–Child Relationships and the Parents' Relationships with Their Parents

Besides their experiences with siblings, young parents can draw on their experiences with their own parents. Young parents are likely to remember a lot of what their parents have done to them and to their siblings during their childhood and youth. They could not prevent those memories from affecting their ideas of a good family life even if they tried to. The manner, time, and duration of their daily get-togethers, the things they did and talked about; the views of family life, work, and school that were expressed; the ways visitors were received and visits paid; the way one ate, went to bed, woke up, and spent the weekend—all are engrained in the young parents.

The spouses' memories of their respective parents and of their many dealings with them can be quite different and sometimes give rise to conflicts between the spouses. When the parents of one spouse resemble the parents of the other — when, say, the fathers of both are strong and the mothers soft and submissive; when the milieu was about the same; when both sets of parents come from similar professions or social strata; when they are alike in ethnic origin, philosophy of life or religion, education and language — the young couple ordinarily find it quite easy to tune their expectations of family life to each other's.

The situation may be quite different when there are discrepancies in the two families' education, when their ethnic background is not the same or when they do not even speak the same language, or when the parents of one partner have a reverse authority relationship — when, for example, in one family the mother was and is the leading and dominating personality, father the kind and self-effacing helper.

In that way, the spouses' ideas of what their family life should be like and how their children should be raised might clash. Which parent should bear the primary responsibility of childrearing and which should defer to the other will continue to be an issue of contention for the parents, and will have an impact on the growing children as well. The controversy may expand to the evaluation of men and women in general as well as to the spouses' and their families' respective achievements in life. Sometimes the spouses' parents join the fights.

As they do in the marriage partners' relationships with their children, sibling positions obviously matter in the partners' relationships with each other and with their own parents. The reader is reminded, though, that similarity or identity in the sibling positions of a spouse and his same-sex parent tends to reinforce his sibling role. An identification conflict between a spouse and his parent, on the other hand, is likely to weaken the characteristics of his sibling role. This may be good or bad for the spouses. When by virtue of their sibling roles they would be in conflict with each other (for example (s)b/(b)s), weakening of the sibling role, say of the husband's (because his father was the oldest brother of sisters), may mitigate the spouses' conflict. On the other hand, complementarity of the spouses' sibling roles (for instance b(s)/(b)s) could be aggravated by identification conflicts of the spouses with their same-sex parents. The husband's father could, for example, have been a younger brother of sisters, the wife's mother the oldest sister of brothers. Both spouses might then vacillate in their interactions with each other and with their children, between what their own sibling roles taught them to feel and do and what their same-sex parents would have done or have wanted them to do.

Single children have had no sibling experience in their original family. They can draw only on their experiences with their parents. The emotional ties to their parents often stay stronger and their dependence on them is often more evident than is the case with other spouses. Yet they may also be more identified with them and more likely to know and heed their wishes. More often than other spouses they want only one child—again following their parents' example.

Through identification with their same-sex parent, single children also assume characteristics of the sibling role of that parent. If the same-sex parent was an oldest sibling, the single child is more likely than other single children to practice responsibility and care in a family of his own. If that parent was a youngest sibling, the single child is more likely to leave leadership and nurture of the children to the spouse and to want even more care for himself than do other parents. If the same-sex parent was himself or herself a single child, the singleton characteristics of the single child will be enhanced.

Other Influences in Parent–Child Relationships

Besides the influences of family structure there are constitutional and inherited characteristics that influence parent–child relationships: looks and height, physical, technical, social, linguistic, scientific, or artistic talents, endurance, frustration tolerance, and temperament.

Constitutional factors and special talents correlate moderately among siblings as well as between parents and children. This implies a fair amount of variation within a sibling configuration regardless of sibling position or family structure. If one parent has scientific and athletic talents and the other artistic, linguistic, and social talents, there is no telling whether paternal or maternal characteristics will dominate among the children, whether paternal and maternal talents may combine in one child, whether only one parent's talents may appear in another child (albeit to a very high degree), and whether none of the parents' talents may show in a third child. This child, however, may display a gift that had not been observed in either parent: an uncanny skill in dealing with mathematical symbols, say, or, an extraordinary memory for visual detail.

Innate characteristics like those may create special positions for children or a parent that outweigh and even suppress influences of family structure. If one or both parents had artistic ambitions that they were never able to realize, and one of their three children, perhaps the youngest, shows exceptional artistic talents, this child may be favored by the parents so much that it eventually exceeds both older siblings in power and influence. If this youngest sibling is a girl and the older siblings are boys, they may even gain the impression that boys and men are of lesser importance in this world than little girls.

A child's resemblances to another family member—a similarity in looks, for example, to a paternal grandfather (who happened to be, say, a distinguished politician or founder of a family enterprise) or in temperament to the mother or maternal grandmother, who has always looked after the family—may favor that child or possibly pressure it into an unsuitable social life or professional career. The child may, for example, take over the family firm, although other children are also interested in and better qualified for the job. Or, in the second case, the mother or grandmother raises the child to be her successor in overseeing all family matters in spite of the fact that she is the youngest and her siblings don't accept her in that role.

Finally, there are customs and conventions that favor certain positions in the family, such as being the first-born and male. Successions in larger estates or inherited political functions, as in monarchies and dukedoms, are examples. Farms are frequently passed on to the oldest son and to daughters only when they marry a farmer.

Beyond institutional preferences, such as first-born and male children, that govern at least some areas of a population's life, there is another biological and sociological component to consider: through pregnancy, gestation, breast-feeding, and nurturing, mothers are usually tied more intimately and closely to their children than are men who, after all, cannot always be sure that they are even the fathers.

As a result of these close bonds between mothers and their children that form before birth and during the first months of the child's extrauterine life mothers become the more natural and graceful attendants of their children than men. Fathers may imitate this ceaseless mother–child inter-action, but they usually have less skill and patience than mothers—except in those families in which the mother has ambivalent feelings toward her child and/or toward the child's father. Such mothers don't fully want their child, feel unloved by their husband, or think that they have chosen the wrong man in the first place.

Be that as it may, in most families mothers spend substantially more time with their children than do fathers. If a mother had a job before she got pregnant and eventually wants to return to it, she has usually been out of the job market for ten or more years. She has been waiting until her youngest child has entered kindergarten or school and takes on part-time jobs at first. Only five to ten years later will she begin to work full time again.

That means, however, that motherhood puts a woman at a disadvantage, especially in the professions and often causes her to feel underprivileged. On the other hand, employers in business as well as in public institutions cannot reasonably be expected to ignore a mother's long absence from work. Such women will have to resume work where they left off ten or more years ago. Some are able to make up for their deficit in experience and competence that has accumulated through the years of mothering, but as a rule they do not earn as much as men do nor even as much as those women who never quit to become mothers, but rather stay on the job. In short, despite the justified strivings of women for emancipation they, rather than men, will still likely be the inheritors of household and mother roles for several more years. As things stand, women will continue to make the choice between motherhood and a profession. They can hardly ever do both at the same time—except for those few women who, because of their own economic resources or those of their husbands or because of their very high professional qualifications (earned before they became mothers), can finance a governess or permanent substitute mother for their children. Other exceptions are, perhaps, those women who manage to involve their own parents or those of their husbands in rearing their children. In some farms and other family enterprises this is still happening today. In all such instances, however, women must be prepared to recognize that the substitute mothers they have recruited over time become the true mothers of their children, psychologically speaking.

These differential privileges of men and women in their respective careers is another important influence whose effects can be seen early in children's lives. Yet this influence can be negligible, the better the mutual understanding is between the parents and the more they are reconciled to their life situation and its opportunities.

Losses of Family Members

One of ten families is likely to have lost a parent or a sibling before a child has turned 15 or 16 years of age. A very early loss of a parent, a loss that is within the first six years of life, is suffered by one out of twenty families. This includes a parent missing from birth on; such a missing parent usually is the father. In certain segments of the population (for example, the lower class, economically speaking, or families with juvenile delinquents) early losses of family members are considerably more frequent (Toman 1974, 1976, Toman and Preiser 1973).

The earlier in life the loss of persons with whom one has lived occurs, the more traumatic the loss. We propose on the basis of many years of clinical-psychological experience to call the loss of a family member, particularly a parent, *very grave* when it occurs during the first six years of life; we call it *grave* when it occurs in a person's late childhood or early youth, that is, between 7 and 16 years of age.

Grave and very grave losses have traumatic consequences. Grave losses increase the likelihood of neurotic personality development, very grave losses, that of psychotic or criminal personality development, even when family life itself does not seem too disrupted. Losses of family members suffered after a person has turned 16, however, as a rule no longer have traumatic effects on personality development. Overcoming even these losses takes time and mourning, to be sure, but they rarely result in permanent psychological disturbances. They do not increase the likelihood of neurosis, delinquency, criminality, or psychosis.

The best remedy for losing a parent is replacement or substitution. A lost father can best be compensated for by another man who enters the family and assumes his position, a lost mother best by a stepmother. The more the substitute person resembles the lost person, the easier it is to integrate this substitute person into the family. If the substitute happens to be a relative—perhaps the lost father's brother or the lost mother's sister or cousin—or a friend who has been in touch with the family all along, his acceptance will ordinarily be quicker. Usually substitute persons are not easy to come by, though, and a family has to be content with a person of little resemblance to the person lost. Thus, integration into the family takes longer.

Even a person who is very similar to the lost person cannot take that person's place at once. He or she has to get to know the family, and the lost person has to be mourned over and inwardly relinquished in all aspects of the family's life. Only when the work of mourning has been completed (Freud 1916) are family members ready to accept another person.

When no substitute person can be recruited, the surviving or remaining family members somehow try to take over the tasks and functions of the lost person. Older siblings become more fatherly or motherly toward their younger siblings to soften the effects of parental loss. They can do this more easily, the more siblings there are. If a sibling rather than a parent is lost, another sibling might adopt that person's position, too. Sometimes the loss of a child will cause parents to have another child.

Subjectively the loss of a parent appears to be graver for

the surviving parent than for any of the children. After all, the lost partner had been chosen by the surviving parent of his own free will, whereas the children had no option of siblings or parents to speak of. With a love and marriage partner, however, one not only agrees on starting life together, but also on shaping that life, including having and raising children. Moreover, there are intimate experiences with the spouse that tend to surpass in satisfaction and fulfillment all familiarities and intimacies encountered as a child in one's family of origin. The loss of a spouse may, therefore, be felt extremely deeply, but its objective effects are likely to be less than a young child's loss of a parent. A spouse can also find ways to make up for the loss. The adult can, after a period of mourning, look for a new partner. Such a search is more difficult, the older the surviving partner has become and the greater the number of children. Potential partners of fitting age become increasingly rare. Either they are already married, or they are single, either because they could not marry—their beloved was already married or did not reciprocate the feelings—or because they did not want to marry. Thus, we may assume that people are not being disrupted in their personality development by the loss of a spouse. In fact, their personality development probably has by then been completed.

There is a similar gap between subjective experience and objective effects when it comes to the loss of one's child. Since parents have generated their child themselves and the child has been utterly dependent on them, they inevitably feel at fault when the child is suffering pain and even more so when it dies, regardless of how innocent they may be objectively. They feel strongly that they have not done enough for the child.

Mourning with guilt feelings, however, is prolonged mourning. Ambivalence toward a lost person—hatred or fear mixed with positive feelings—creates guilt feelings vis-à-vis that person. One may have wished for that person's loss or demise, if only unconsciously. Hence one does not really dare to mourn. One does not seek out those situations or remember past events in which the lost person had participated in order to establish emotionally for oneself that the person will no longer be present in such situations and events—rather, one avoids them. Only when one happens to come up unexpectedly, can one go on working at mourning, guilt feelings or not. For those reasons parents who have lost a child suffer for a long time. Nevertheless, they are hardly jeopardized in coping with life. They can even work towards substitution; they can generate another child.

Replacement of lost family members, which implies step-parents, sometimes step-siblings too, creates problems of integration into the family. When a person who has not yet had a family becomes a substitute parent, he or she may not know how to muster the necessary patience and care to gain the children's trust. If a substitute parent has already been a parent in a family of his own, he does bring along experience but might lack interest in his new stepchildren. His heart may rather be with his own children. When such a substitute parent brings his own children along, the problems incurred grow in proportion to the number of children. In a healthy life together everyone should establish a positive relationship with everyone else. Yet the two groups of children are inclined to cling to their own siblings and turn against the other group. Their attachment to the remaining natural parent also increases in intensity. At the same time, they are worried about the future. If they have lost a parent and the other parent has turned to a new person, could they lose that new person, too, one day? Could they even lose their remaining parent? Such are their anxieties.

When a remarried couple (each partner with children from a previous marriage) have children with each other, the uncertainty and confusion of the existing children grow even

greater. Now they all have one real parent and one stepparent, whereas their newborn half-siblings have two real
(natural) parents. They fear their parents will try one day to
shed the children from their first marriages and keep only
their common natural children.

The loss of a natural parent through separation or
divorce (rather than through death) more likely adds to the
children's conflicts and doubts. The children don't know
whether they should keep up some kind of relationship with
the absent parent. Perhaps he is in fact the dearer parent, in
spite of the court's ruling. When, incidentally, such a parent
is exercising visitation rights, the loss to the child is psychologically considered a *partial loss* of the parent. Contact with
that parent may be quite reduced and sporadic, but it has not
stopped entirely.

When such a separated or divorced parent returns to
the family, we are dealing with a *temporary loss*. Like the
permanent loss of a parent, it is graver in its psychological
effects, the earlier in the child's life it occurred and the longer
it lasted before the lost parent returned. A temporary loss of
long duration is experienced like a permanent loss. After
such a long absence, it may be hard to accept the returning
parent again; he has become a stranger. The more contact
with the family an absent parent has maintained, the less he
has been lost to the family psychologically. When a long-
absent parent returns and a substitute partnership entered
into by the remaining parent breaks up, this, too, constitutes
a loss in the children's minds. Its effects are less, however,
the later this stepparent entered the life of the children and
the shorter he stayed.

When a *parent* was *lost through death*, the situation is
different in several ways. A dead parent can help the
children no longer. On the other hand, the majority of such
deaths are acts of fate, caused by illness or accidents,
sometimes by wars. The parents did not want to part; the

lost parent did not wish to leave the family. Usually, he will be more dearly remembered than a parent who just left. What's more, the parents and siblings of the deceased parent are more likely to remain interested in and available to the family of the deceased than when a parent has left the family of his own free will. In the latter case the departing parent's family of origin, too, had often not been interested in his family, or merely antagonistically so, even while he was still around.

After a loss of a family member, recruiting a substitute for the lost person is usually the best solution and staying together without recruiting a substitute the second best. Mobilizing an occasional helper, perhaps from the surviving parent's family of origin or from friends, is better than having no substitute.

A split in the family would be among the poorer solutions. It would mean more losses of family members for the afflicted. Still less desirable would be a complete break-up, in which family members end up with different adoptive or foster families. The worst solution, however, would ordinarily be to transfer each of the children to a different home or institution where not even a semblance of family structure is provided.

Not only do one's personal losses have adverse psychological effects, even those suffered by the parents in their early lives are often passed on as it were to the child. Losses of family members teach the bereaved that losses are possible. Dear persons may be taken away at any time; more losses may be forthcoming.

The duplication theorem (Toman 1961, 1965, 1971) as applied to losses implies just that: the afflicted learns to anticipate losses. He who has suffered them feels comparatively safer in view of the possibility of losses than without it. He understands and chooses for friends people who have suffered losses themselves—and he chooses more anxiously and poorly to begin with. He is so happy that somebody will take to him at all, he may not see the conflicts that he is getting himself into in the process. He clings to persons who do not mean very much to him and could, if need be, leave again. More often than aligning with people who have suffered no losses, he chooses friends and partners who will not stay with him but, rather, leave him early and unexpectedly (Toman 1961, 1965). He shows little optimism for life, enters permanent partnerships later than others, and is more hesitant about having children. He or she has them later and in slightly smaller numbers, statistically speaking, than persons who have not suffered losses of family members (Toman 1974, 1976).

What remains to be clarified are the implications of a family member's being missing from the start. There is no transition from the presence of a family member to his permanent absence and, consequently, no suffering over it, no mourning, and no eventual search for a substitute. Is it not better to have never had a father than to have had one but lost him?

The answer is no. The child who never had a father does not miss him, to be sure, but he grows up with the feeling that there are no fathers or fatherlike creatures. Consequently, he does not search for a father. Yet father-like people are a fact of life. They are integral parts of our social and professional realities. Without the experience of contact with a father figure at home, a person usually cannot adequately develop relationships with people in positions of authority outside the family. He is in for considerable trouble. In contrast, a person losing a father or a mother after having enjoyed him or her at least for a few years suffers pain, but the bereaved's developmental prognosis is better.

This holds for siblings too. Single children do not know what they are missing. A child that has had a sibling but lost him or her and now feels alone, knows what he is missing and is looking for a replacement. Since life with other people, especially with peers, is an inescapable social reality, the single child has a deficit of experience and interest. One could call the one-child family – with caution, please, compensations are possible – the mildest form of an incomplete family.

THE GROWTH OF FAMILY LIFE

A happy family life depends, among other things, on loving parents who are pleased with each other, on the existence of children, preferably more than one, and on joyful and considerate relationships with those children. Caring parents do not only express their own wishes but know those of other family members as well and consider them almost as important or even equally important as their own – and sometimes even more important. The instinctive and emotional pleasure that their children give to them, just by being what they are, is usually great enough that parents gladly take on the burden of their care and education, and the attending worries and tests of patience. Occasionally the parents would love some relief, but they don't really evade the work of childrearing. They don't want to leave the family even when professional, economic, and social opportunities are often drawing them away. They do not leave spouse and children for long stretches of time. When they are temporarily separated, they stay in touch via telephone calls and letter writing. If unavoidable separations are long, they make room for short homecomings. They remain interested in family affairs and what each family member is doing and thinking; they hope that there won't be essential changes in family life while they are away, or at least that they are being duly informed and consulted and that anything unfortunate that has happened can still be influenced when they get back. They, the parents, stay in touch with their children and try to make time for them whenever possible.

Childhood

In an atmosphere like that just described, children can move without serious disappointments through the various phases of childhood. There are basically three such phases:

- A period of utter dependence on the parents, mostly the mother; also called the *oral* or *passivity phase* (Erikson 1950, Freud 1916–1917, Portmann 1956, et al.). It occupies about the first year of life.

- A period of beginning autonomy, of active locomotion and increasing power struggles with the mother and other family members. It is called the *anal* or *activity phase* (Freud 1916–1917, Erikson et al. 1950). Ordinarily it extends through the second and third year of life.

- A period of identifying oneself (as a boy or as a girl, among others) and of developing sex specific relationships with family members and other persons around. On account of the growing sexual and love interests of the child it has also been called the (early) genital phase, and on account of the interchanges with father and mother as man and woman, also the *oedipal* or *love phase* (Freud 1916–1917, Erikson 1950). It lasts through about the fourth and fifth year of life.

The Oral or Passivity Phase

In the oral or passivity phase (the first year of life) the child starts out with waking periods of half an hour to an hour, whereupon it goes to sleep again for three or more hours. A few weeks after birth it begins to skip one of those waking periods during the night, usually to the relief of the parents. The waking periods now gradually get longer.

During such waking periods the child is being fed, cleaned, and changed and is developing its senses and sensuous contacts with its guardian (usually the mother) and its world. Within four to six months the many and increasingly subtle and intricate contacts with the mother lead to the child's ability to distinguish her from other persons who greet it or who may occasionally join in the child's care. The child loves those sensuous contacts. It may, for example, laugh and scream with impatience when it needs Mother again and sees her coming. It learns to treasure the attending person; the tastes and smells she engenders, the touches she provides, and the handling she offers. It learns to love the sight and sound of her. This love started with the child's infatuation with Mother's breast (or, second best, with Mother's bottle), but gradually it expands to include more and more of the entire person and all the stimulations that emanate from her.

During the first four to six months of life the attending person could still be replaced without too much trouble by another truly caring person. After that time this becomes no longer possible without hurting the child severely. It might suffer a grave loss that could even cause the child to die (Spitz 1957). The attending person has become the mother, even if the child is not hers.

During the second half of the first year the child gets more and more thoroughly used to the attending person. It experiences her as an all-loving, all-giving person who imposes no conditions and is happy when the child lives and moves, eats and eliminates. She is like a good fairy, a goddess or a god. The gender of the attending person does not yet matter to the child, even though the services of a female nurse happen to be ordinarily better than those of a male nurse. This holds true even more when there is a strong and spontaneous interest in the child, as may be expected of the child's natural parents. Even with adoptive parents, the mother is usually the better nurse. In the case of a physical inability to have children, it often was the wife who pressed for adoption of a child, rather than the husband.

By the end of the first year of life the child can handle simple objects like dolls, rattles, and spoons and cooperate with the feeding and caretaking person. It can sit, crawl, rock, and stand up. It is on the verge of leaving the crib and roaming around the home of its own accord. It understands a few spoken words among the many that mother uses in her talks to the baby. Those words have assumed meaning for the child; most other words and spoken utterances are understood only vaguely. They make the music to the child's physical interactions with mother.

The Anal or Activity Phase

In the anal or activity phase (the second and third year of life) the child is increasingly getting in the way of other family members, particularly its older siblings. Their possessions are no longer safe from this stumbling, restless little creature. There is a need to regulate behavior. The mildest solution is to remove the opportunity for infringements — say, by hiding or locking away the dearest or most fragile of one's possessions. One can also enter into negotiations with the child. It ought to learn to make concessions, that is, to give something in return when it wants to get something.

During the second year the child becomes able to express itself in two- and three-word sentences which, however, tend to be baby-talk and intelligible only to family members. By the end of the third year, however, the child is usually speaking clearly enough to be intelligible to outsiders. The child's utterances can now be many words long. Combinations and subordinations of sentences are possible (e.g., "Jack is leaving, because he does not want to play"). The child is even using personal pronouns properly and referring to itself by saying "I" (not: "Jack is leaving," but: "I is (am) leaving").

It is reasonable to expect that with such language facility the child should now be able to negotiate power and ownership conflicts. Competition with family members, achievement, competence, and the acquisition or creation of goods (such as getting a doll, ordering toys, or painting a picture) play an increasing part in the child's struggles with family members. Beyond competition there are partisanships and alliances, in which the powers that people have matter, whereas their gender does not.

During the anal or activity phase the child also learns cleanliness. In the parents' interactions with the child's behavior in elimination (which are about as frequent and time consuming to parents as the interactions over eating were or still are), the child recognizes the parents' (and older siblings') interests and intentions with respect to its bladder and bowel movements. The child can announce them more and more accurately, gains control over them, and can even use them, by holding back or letting go at inopportune moments – to blackmail the parents. By the end of the third year, as a rule, the child is toilet trained. He needs diapers neither during the day nor at night. Mishaps have become rare.

The Oedipal or Love Phase

The oedipal or love phase stretches through about the fourth and fifth years of the child's life. In addition to the pleasures of eating, watching, listening, and bodily touch (all first secured during the oral phase), and those of running, jumping, handling and throwing, etc., as well as eliminating bodily waste (all developed first during the anal phase), the child is now discovering the pleasures of sexual (genital) stimulation and activity (Freud 1905, 1916–1917). The child is becoming not only interested in his own sex organs, but, more secretively, also in those of its parents and siblings. It learns about the anatomical sex differences between male and female and identifies itself as a boy or girl, and each parent as a man or woman. Until then it may have believed that a child can elect its own sex. From now on the child relates increasingly differently toward family members and other persons depending upon whether they are of the same or the opposite sex than he or she.

The boy restricts his strivings for achievement and superiority more or less to males. In contrast, females are courted, presented with gifts and favors; one does what they want. They are attractive; one wants to win their interest and affection. Only those females who are unattractive to him may be treated the way he treats males.

The girl, too, constrains her rivalry feelings to persons of her own sex. At first she may be struck by a certain envy of boys (for being boys and having what makes them boys). Sooner or later, however, she tends to overcome this. If she cannot be a boy, she will at least be able to have boys for friends and suitors. And if her sex organ is not as articulate and conspicuous as is that of a boy, she will be able to do something that boys can never do: she can have children.

How children are conceived, what parents do with each other when they are by themselves, how they (the children) have come about—these are the puzzles that increasingly fascinate children. They keep asking questions about them, especially when parents or other informed persons convey the impression that they are willing to talk about those things. The boy may wonder, moreover, about the possibilities of removing Father and keeping Mother for himself, the girl about how she and Father could get together now and then and leave out Mother. Such wishes or fantasies of doing away with the same-sex parent (first described in Freud 1900, 1916–1917) are practically inevitable, just as they are vis-à-vis newborn siblings. At first many children think that siblings should go back where they came from. In a favorable family milieu, however, such wishes and fantasies can soon be overcome. Ultimately, the child is happy to have and keep both parents, just as it is about keeping the later-born siblings, even when at times they are annoying. The loss of a parent would be in the long run no wish fulfillment, but rather a trauma.

As we have mentioned, boys identify with their fathers, girls with their mothers. This identification helps children to cope with demands on the parents that cannot be fulfilled. When a boy does not get everything from Mother that Father seems to get from her, he can at least become like Father. That way Mother may be a bit more generous toward him after all. When a father loves his daughter but loves his wife even more, the daughter can increase her chances with Father when she becomes like Mother. Parents seem to treasure such identifications of their children with the same-sex parent.

Late Childhood and Early Youth

The period of late childhood and early youth has been called the *latency period* by Freud (1916–1917) because sexual interest in the parents and siblings moves into the background in the child's mind. This phase lasts from about 6 to 12 years of age and ends with puberty. The child is out of the parental home for increasingly longer time stretches a day, usually for several hours. He or she goes to kindergarten and later to school, and stays at playgrounds under slight or no supervision by the parents. Occasional separations from the family may extend to a full day and still be tolerated but ordinarily not more than that unless the child has been mentally prepared for it well in advance and preferably step by step. The child should be in the company of a familiar person, if at all possible a family member, for several hours at least or for the whole first day of such a longer sojourn away from home. The more familiar the persons are to the child, however, (like uncle, aunt, or grandparents), the less the need for such a transitional presence of a nuclear family member.

Some children have to get used to the absence of parents as early as in late childhood or even sooner in their lives. Both parents may be working and may put the child in a day-care center; or the children may see their parents only on weekends. Such conditions are hard on children. To the extent that they do get used to them, children may become estranged from their parents. The people with whom they spend most of their time are slowly becoming important in their lives. Their parents may change psychologically into something like an uncle and aunt.

Even more traumatic is the loss of parents and the child's transfer to foster parents. If such losses occur at a time when the child has begun nursery or elementary school, those institutions could help him to cope with the loss and with the necessary adjustment to foster parents. Teachers, classmates, and sometimes even their parents can stand by the child and try to understand its sorrow. At least school stays the same, the child may feel with relief. If, however, the child has to switch schools at the same time, the child's situation may become even more devastating. At any rate, the real work of overcoming the loss goes on in the new home.

On the whole, school is still less important and influential than home. This observation can be derived from the fact, among others, that school phobia—that is, a fear of school or the child's refusal to go to or stay in school—usually proves to be a fear not so much of school but of what happens at home while the child is in school. The child is not sure of its parents or its home. He has doubts about the parents' love for each other and for him, their child. A family member may run away. The child may find its home closed upon returning. The family may break up or disappear.

Under favorable circumstances the child, during latency, is enormously expanding its knowledge of the world and of people outside the family. The linguistic, intellectual, and motor development at ages 11 and 12 reaches the level of young adults, even if the exercise of their abilities and the construction of an adult reality concept—in which objectivity, truth, honesty, or at least loyalty and causal explanations matter— are only beginning. Emotional development, on the other hand, flattens during the latency period. It is not so much feelings as factual connections between people and things that concern and absorb him. This changes in puberty.

At 11 or 12 years of age, the youngster can do without its parents for long weekends and even for weeks, as long as he or she is in the company of friends. He does not even have to be familiar with his companions at the start. A summer camp, a hostel or vacation home, a group hike with new youngsters does not scare him any more. The others are in the same boat; they are also away from home.

Adolescence

In puberty the young person gets concerned, even upset, over the comparatively rapid bodily and hormonal changes he or she is going through. More is happening inside them than ever before, they feel. More so than in the oedipal phase they experience sexual urges and emotional, sensual, and intellectual interests whose objects they don't know yet. Parents and siblings cannot completely fulfill these needs, but even persons known to them from school and playgrounds are taboo because of long contact with them; they are no candidates for love. Somebody less familiar or even a perfect stranger, though, can fascinate them. The parents usually don't object too much when that person or that person's family (or at least his or her place of origin) are known to them. The adolescent may seek contact with that person, contact, however, should not be too frequent or intensive, the parents believe. The adolescent should not engage in intimate relations until he, or she, knows that the person is right, and school, work, sports, etc. would not suffer.

These are the parents' (and sometimes also the older siblings') hopes. When the adolescent's idol or love is not from the neighborhood, when that person's origin is quite different or unknown, when he or she is much older, when his or her means of livelihood, professional background, or long-term plans are obscure, the parents tend to object more strongly. They are particularly wary when several persons at once are involved—when people of questionable reputation or a gang of delinquents is attracting their children. They express their concern, question their child's wisdom, or forbid outright all contacts under risk of sanctions.

Under favorable circumstances—that is, when the youngster is in love with a person whom the parents on the whole approve of, he or she does not immediately jump into bed with that person. During the first two or three years after puberty has started, young people tend to talk a lot about love and learn about it from books, movies, and radio and television rather than practice it in reality. This holds at least for adolescents in intact families living under reasonably secure circumstances. During that time the parents may, however, have to put up with platonic illusions, autoerotic practices, and even sexual interest in persons of the same sex. Where these arise, they are likely to be of short duration.

Heterosexual interests prevail, as a rule, as soon as there are realistic opportunities.

During the years of puberty and adolescence, most young people experience the pleasures of heterosexual relations. By the age of 19 or 20, the great majority of all young men and women have started having sexual relationships or have at least tried to. Young women are more likely to feel attracted to just one man than are young men to just one woman. Even men, however, are capable of and interested in monogamous bonds. It all depends on the partners' compatibility with such things as physical appearance, language, education, social background, interests and talents, ethnic, philosophical, or religious orientation as well as experiences and roles in the family of origin and with early friends.

While the young partners are not yet married or living together, their intimate contacts with each other may be subjected to social and practical obstructions. The parents are not exactly delighted; even their childrens' own rooms are not really designed for intimate sexual contacts. The adolescent should not lock himself up in his room, let alone when he's with a friend. This holds true even when the parents grant him privacy and would certainly knock at the door before entering. No, for a while longer, adolescent lovers may have to go into hiding for their intimate relationships or search for opportunities in the homes of friends, in adolescent communes, on camping trips, in protected places in the open air, in hotel rooms or, as observed in the housing-short Soviet Union, in sleeping cars of trains. Young lovers there travel one night to Leningrad, for instance, and return the next night.

Adolescence is not all love relationships. In fact, they consume only a fraction of their time. Adolescents are also occupied with school, jobs, and friends, and are involved with individual or group sports, cars, dancing, and music, etc. The young person is slowly growing into the adult world and, despite initial protests and identity crises (Erikson 1959), beginning to view the world more and more the way grownups do. He no longer imitates idols whose behavior the parents often did not understand. Rather, he incorporates the various roles he assumed on a trial basis—his identifications with model persons—into his own personality. Now he knows what he wants, and his life, friendship, love, and professional goals are no longer contradicting each other. They have become compatible.

Leaving the Family of Origin

From childhood on a person becomes more independent from its family for progressively longer stretches of time. People outside the family assume growing importance. Eventually, sometimes during the latency period, but more often in puberty and adolescence, persons outside the family may temporarily and subjectively become even more important than the dearest of family members. Being in love for the first time often comes like a revelation to the adolescent. All previous loves fade in comparison. This feeling does not last, though. One's first great love passes. Either it becomes more sober and objective or it changes into a permanent state of loving partnership. It may also end altogether. Disappointed and a bit wiser, he or she may cautiously try again after a while.

Within the family there are forces and motives at work that can further or hinder children's excursions into the outside world. Usually parents let their youngsters move away as far and for as long as they please. Parents apply brakes only if they think their child can't do what it set out to do; they want to save it from disappointments. If they are afraid that he may otherwise stick too close to home and cling to them, they encourage him to be a little more adventurous away from home.

Parents do want their children to become independent—not overnight, but gradually—and they want to know how the children have been faring in their attempts. On the other hand, they want to keep their children; they don't want to lose them to other people. Both parental motives are normal. Their respective satisfactions and the compromises between them have to be worked out with their children time and again. As all involved get more experienced, negotiations become streamlined and are often even omitted. A tacit understanding emerges. Only when the youngsters want too much freedom and independence or when because of their disappointments they try to withdraw to a little enclave outside the family, do arguments arise and new negotiations take place.

When a family has several children, it is easier for parents to let them go than when they have only one or two. When the first goes, the others will stay with them for a while. That helps. When the second goes, it's easier because of the experience with the first, and when the last one goes, they may already have grandchildren who are returning. Only if, say, the only girl among several boys is leaving, or the only boy among several girls, may the parents feel somewhat more upset.

Leaving home is not an undivided pleasure for the children, either. Later-born children are likely, however, to take the departure of the oldest as an example. They may even get encouragement from their sister or brother as well as some help at the start. With all of them it is understood, though, that they are not leaving forever; they come back for visits. Often they retain their rooms in the parental home, or at least their bed and closet.

Frequently children depend at first on financial support from parents. When they are still in school or in training, their dependence on parents is drastic and may be trouble-some. Along with providing material help, the parents may continue to exercise some control over their sons and daughters. They want to know what their children are doing with the money and may try to steer them in certain directions. When parents don't do that, they may well have been intimidated by their children, friends, or legal authorities, or they are really indifferent. They may give their children money in order to be rid of them. When parents do not or cannot afford financial support for their children's higher or continued education, institutions may offer stipends or loans.

Even the longest courses of education end one day. Many young people stop training before they are 20. Those with academic careers typically continue until 25 or 30 years of age and may already be living in their own home with a partner or spouse. They may even have a child and are probably in transition to independence. Many of them are longing for ultimate autonomy, even if it will take several more years to repay the debts they have incurred to finance their studies.

Only a few of them never reach a state of self-support that had, after all, been the hope of their parents, relatives, and friends along with the subsidizing public. They believe that they will continue to study forever and that society owes them a living. After all, they never asked to be born. What they want is to read and chat, to make love and rest, to drink and smoke, and perhaps to "get a fix" when the ordinary pleasures of the day have come to feel shallow. They are the future charges of social workers, psychotherapists, or probation officers, and often not even they can help them.

Most of those "long-term trainees" succeed in their strivings toward self-support and professional commitment. They find a partner for life, marry with help from the government and/or the family, and do want to do things themselves from now on. A certain amount of contact with the parents is usually retained. The parents' help in little things, especially with small children, is appreciated. Yet such help should be moderate and unconditional.

DISRUPTIONS IN FAMILY DEVELOPMENT

In this developmental process that extends from the choice of a spouse and the birth of children all the way to the exodus of those children and the founding of their own families, there are many ways in which it can go wrong. So numerous are the possibilities of disruption, in fact, and so obtrusive in some instances, that a scientific observer may wonder how new families are ever formed and why so many people are apparently trying and succeeding. We might assume that there are basic biological, psychological, and societal forces at work.

The need for care and love in the small child, the heterosexual love interests and sexual needs of young people and adults, and the instinct to respond with nurture, care, and love to babies and children—something to which women on the average are more immediately susceptible than men, though men are not devoid of it either—represent important biological components (Harlow 1958, Lorenz 1939, 1943, 1952, Tinbergen 1951, 1953).

Psychological forces are rooted in the multitude of experiences that humans are having and automatically organizing in their minds and from which they can transfer, generalize, and abstract onto other, new situations, and in the uniquely human ability to talk about those experiences with others (Bühler 1930, Chomsky 1957, Freud 1900, 1916-1917, Hilgard and Bower 1966, Hörmann et al. 1970, Hull 1943, Jung 1912, Tolman 1932).

Societal forces institutionalize biological and psychological forces in all kinds and forms of social life and generate customs, rituals, and laws, that further the long-term goals of the group, among which perpetuation of the group and its offspring seem to be nonnegotiable. Where a group has foregone that goal, it perishes before long. This is true of families, clans, tribes or of an entire people. The group will not continue to exist; its individuals will be scattered and absorbed, or they will die.

In spite of such basic biological, psychological, and societal forces that (among others) support family life and family development, there are many pitfalls. Choices of partners can be unfortunate. The lovers or spouses discover before long that they are not getting from each other what they had hoped for, and conflicts ensue. These may be based on differences in ethnic or class origins, in religion, or in levels of education. Even when there are no such differences, spouses may be incompatible because of physical appearance and constitution, temperament, basic needs, and interests, including their sexual desires and emotional needs. This does not mean that happily married partners may not be different. Certain contrasts make them attractive to each other. When, however, one of them is very vivacious and the other passive and depressed, when one of them loves traveling whereas the other is a homebody, when one adores company and people and the other hates them, there obviously will be conflicts.

Such discrepancies often tend to manifest early in a couple's relationship with each other, but they can be discussed. The partners may conclude in time that they should separate. Sometimes, however, their love and sexual attraction is so intense at first that the conflicts get ignored or overruled. As time goes by, the partners learn that love is not merely sexual attraction, that life together has other aspects and components, and that in terms of time these outweigh the sexual ones. Not even on a honeymoon do sexual intimacies constitute more than a small portion of the young couple's activities and common interests.

Other partner conflicts hinge on their relationships with their parents and siblings. One cannot escape one's parents even when one marries far away from them, without their knowledge or against their strong opposition. Even a wish, such as never to see the parents again is a parental influence. The absence of parents from early life on or the apparent absence of any feelings whatsoever for them is itself a form of parental influence. The same holds for the influences that siblings have exerted on a person and for the role he took within the sibling group. It is of secondary importance whether the relationship with them was good or bad. Even a poor sibling relationship that a person wants to forget and get rid of forces him into various avoidance and denial maneuvers, both within and outside of the family. These are sibling influences, too. Even the missing siblings of a single child may be viewed as a sibling influence.

It should be remembered that a poor sibling relationship is still a familiar one. In a new relationship a person often benefits more from his experience in a poor sibling relationship than from none at all or from trying to pursue the opposite of his sibling relationship.

Influences of Family Members upon Each Other

Parents and siblings affect a person in various ways:

- A relationship within the family of origin may persist long after a person has left the family and established new friendships and acquaintances. For parents a person may always stay the little boy or little girl that he or she once was, or at least the son or daughter; for siblings the older or younger brother or the older or younger sister. Even when things have changed com-

pletely—say, when the parents became old and frail—
they may hold on to their role as parents and feel
responsible and protective toward their children. Older
siblings also try to take care of the younger ones and the
younger ones may look to and lean on older siblings
sometimes long after they have started their own lives.

- Unintentionally, family members serve as models for
new relationships outside the family. This can mean
one of two things: Either one is looking for persons who
closely resemble a family member and is seeking a
relationship in which the partner takes the position of
that family member; thus, a dependent young man
clinging to his parents, perhaps an only child, looks for
a partner who can mother him; or a younger sister longs
for a friend who will treat her as her older brother did at
home. A brother may choose a woman who is gentle
and obedient as his younger sister used to be. In all
those instances one can say that *one transfers an original
family relationship* onto a new person outside the family.

Alternatively, one identifies with a family member
(called the example or model person) and relates to persons
outside the family the way that model person did to a family
member: one treats, for instance, a girlfriend or one's own
child, the way mother treated a younger sister or even
oneself. Put differently, *one transfers an identification relationship* in the family of origin onto a new person outside the
family.

We should note here that a person will more readily
transfer an original family relationship to a new relationship
inside or outside the family, the longer he has held that
relationship in the family and the more successful he was in
practice. The same holds for an identification relationship.
The earlier in life or—more important still, the earlier in his

family of origin—he was able to identify with the model person, the more often he was able to do it and the more successful he was in practice, the sooner he will apply it in a new relationship within or outside the family. Whether a person will succeed with such a transference onto a new relationship depends, of course, on the needs of the other person and, in case of an extrafamilial new relationship, on that person's family of origin.

Needless to say that in many families a person learns and develops more than one kind of relationship when there are several family members, and more than one kind of identification relationship, but he is likely to have practiced some of them more frequently and extensively and learned them better than others. If he applies a less developed kind in a new relationship or if he wavers and switches between several kinds, he may be less successful and, in some instances, appear insincere or unstable to a new family member or a person outside the family. In other instances, however, such efforts of trying different roles may be welcome in the long run. A new family member or an extrafamilial person may like the variety and versatility. It may lead to an increasing adjustment to the other person's needs. It may even preserve and develop a new relationship that was not too compatible to begin with.

Let me give an example of such multiple influences of family members upon each other: A young wife and mother may be unable to shed her child role vis-à-vis her mother. She also chose her husband so that he would cater to her the way her older brother used to; and she may want to be to her child, a daughter, what her mother has been to her. She may strive to be an even better mother and indulge her child in some of the things that were forbidden to her.

Different family members may exert different or identical types of influence. The young wife mentioned may have been encouraged by both her mother and her older brother to submit to and depend on others. They wanted her to be a good little girl, but her father, on the other hand, preferred her to be more independent and motherly. He enjoyed being pampered by women.

Some of this may change in different situations: The young wife mentioned could, for example, be motherly toward her child when she is alone with her, but may throw up her arms as soon as her own mother is visiting and approaching the child. The mother feels that she can take control of the child as she pleases. The same young wife may be submissive and childish toward her husband, yet caring and guiding in her interaction with one of her girlfriends.

With respect to a particular person or in a given situation a person may change his or her behavior. Our young wife may become more dominant and self-assured when dealing with her husband. What her father had wanted from her and had gotten from her mother she may eventually be able to give her husband, although she may have imagined a different kind of life with him at first. The identification with her mother, which she expressed with her child, comes in handy also in her new relationship with her husband.

All these processes are unconscious or only partly conscious. Influences exerted by the family of origin are natural and inevitable. They are applied inadvertently and intuitively to new persons and situations. Upon reflection one can, if need be, think about those applications and possibly recognize the principles behind them. In a new situation, however, one is rarely aware of these principles and that may be just as well. The new situation can be contemplated better in retrospect than in the immediate present, and whatever lessons are drawn from it occurs automatically. The principles sink in, often without notice or explicit statement. One is learning incessantly without being able to tell exactly how and what one is learning. Verbalizing may help, but it is not enough. Having experienced one's actions and their consequences and experiencing them again is what counts. Talking about them afterwards can be useful.

The original family's influences and their applications in new situations with new persons can always be modified. Modifications are necessary because new situations develop and new people respond other than expected. They fit only crudely into the patterns that are being transferred. New people do not want to be merely the ghosts of one's original family members. And what those new people transfer onto oneself does not quite fit either. One is something more than their paradigms. Developing a relationship is a process of continual adaptation and adjustment of one's expectations to the realities of a given partner or friend. The initial transference model is gradually filled out by concrete experiences with the other person and the details learned about him. It is like a skeleton that slowly acquires flesh, blood, and life.

Even that skeleton, the transference model, is not fixed in its structure forever. New aspects of the original model person or model relationship that one transferred onto a new person may retroactively come to the fore. The memory of a kind and permissive father may serve as a woman's paradigm in her choice of a partner. As the relationship with her partner grows, other features of her father image—say that of a protector in situations of danger or that of a counselor when she was puzzled—may emerge, and she will look for these qualities in her partner. A young man whose older sister not only protected, but firmly controlled him may, in the course of his struggles with a lover, remember situations where his sister was helpless and he came to her rescue. He had also been *her* protector, he may realize. As a consequence of these transformations or revisions of the memories concerning the model person, some of the young woman's and young man's partner conflicts may subside. The young woman may accept her spouse's need to assume responsi-

bility and leadership. The young man may play the protector
with his lover or he may accept her independence, her
efficiency, and her mothering without feeling inferior himself.

When friends or partners in love and life do not always
feel comfortable with each other, when they get from each
other only part of what they longed for, when they are rarely
satisfied with one another, the family influences discussed
here may be at the root. Attempts at mutual modification
and adjustment may already have been made but without
the hoped-for result. There are conflicts between the partners. They talk to each other about those conflicts, they talk
with friends, but all that doesn't help much. Meeting with
professional counselors and psychotherapists may be more
useful. As nonpartisan but empathetic observers who have
not been implicated in the couple's daily life, they may be
able to improve the partners' discussions, to articulate their
wishes and to suggest new possibilities of fulfilling them or
of reaching better compromises. Even renunciations of
wishes, should they be found necessary, can be made more
tolerable or palatable than they were at first. One day some
of those renunciations may even be lifted and the wishes
appear fulfillable again. Sometimes such therapeutic discussions and concomitant insights lead to separation of the
partners, perhaps to "separations in friendship," and to a
search for new partners. Conceivably they will make better
choices now than before. If they have no children of their
own yet, this could be considered a favorable outcome. If
they have children, there is more at stake. Separation may
become difficult.

In certain situations children may bring their parents a
bit of relief. This might be the case when, say, two oldest
siblings married each other, are engaged in a struggle for
superiority and leadership, and have not reached sufficient
agreement. When their children arrive, the situation im-

proves. They almost pounce on them with their care and need to guide and may even overdo it. In order to avoid conflict with each other, the parents may have to "divide their children up." The children may possibly have to pledge allegiance to one parent only and sometimes take a position against the other. They are pulled into the leadership struggle of the parents. If the parents have but one child, they may wrestle for its "possession." This causes a lot of turmoil for the child unless one of the parents clearly steps back, leaves the child to the other parent, and tries to lead or take charge somewhere else, perhaps at work.

Apparently, children can be of only limited help when their parents are in conflict with each other. In some instances children clearly increase the parents' conflicts. When both parents have been youngest siblings, for example, each of them is likely to look for leadership, understanding, and care from the other, but the partner cannot provide it. So, they try their luck with their child, who is even less likely to be capable of obliging.

Effects upon the Children in the Family

Conflicts between spouses make them view each other somewhat unrealistically. They still perceive types of persons or types of roles rather than real people, substitute figures for family members and other important people of the past rather than human beings in their own right. The partners transfer old relationships onto the present and thereby learn too little about each other and about the present. They want the other to be what they imagine, not what he or she really is. When the couple has children, they automatically and unconsciously try to influence and mold them in the image of family members or old friends.

They may influence their children's development in three ways:

- The parents cannot hide the conflicts that exist between them from their children. As they grow up and are witnessing these, the children build up an expectation in their minds that the life of men and women together is a troublesome and joyless affair. Such parents spread more strife, anxiety, anger, and hatred in their family than parents without conflicts.

- The parents' conflicts burden the relationship with their children. When they are trying to do well by one parent, the children are not sure whether they are not losing the other parent's approval. They don't know which parent to turn to at times of crisis or separation. Even when their sibling configuration is favorable, the children cannot properly develop their relationships with their parents. When their sibling configuration is not so favorable (say, when there are only boys in the family, or only girls, or when there is a retarded child among them), they are offered few, if any, compensations from the parents for those experiences that they have never had, such as living together with a peer of the opposite sex.

- The child cannot make use of the experiences provided by their siblings. Even a favorable child configuration does not afford them enough opportunity to practice life with peers of the other sex. The parents' conflicts hang like a dark cloud over them; the children remain anxiously tied to one or both parents. When there are only boys or only girls vying unconsciously for the love of the opposite-sex parent, they compete with greater anxiety, hatred, or feelings of guilt than children in families where parents have no conflicts.

When losses of persons occur in a family, particularly when a parent leaves or dies, the remaining parent will of necessity take over the functions of the lost parent. In such a case a mother will become some kind of father, too, and a father will try to act as substitute mother for the child. In that way the children's relationship to their parents is not made any easier. One might think, say that a boy who has lost his father and now has his mother all to himself would be glad about it, and likewise, the girl who lost her mother and keeps her father. The fact is that the remaining parent is now harder put to make ends meet in the house. He or she has less spare time for the children. Even if that is not a problem, the parent is by no means more available to the children or more intimate in dealing with them than he or she was before the other parent was lost.

Whereas children would formerly attribute such constraints imposed on them to the presence of the other parent and his demands on the first one, this rationalization is no longer possible. The remaining parent now seems to impose those constraints and just does not want to be with the child as much as he or she could, the child may feel. The remaining parent does not seem to love the child enough. And what the remaining parent may have let the child do in spite of objections from the other parent, the child is permitted to do no longer, even though the objector is gone. And what the lost parent used to want the child to do in spite of the child's reluctance and the other parent's doubt, the child may now have to do on behalf of the remaining parent. Such things could make life more difficult for the child than when he had both parents.

The loss of the parent of the opposite sex, with the same-sex parent remaining, is even more difficult for the children concerned than is the loss of the same-sex parent. When a family has but one child, the problems are compounded. Then only Father and Son or Mother and Daughter are left. Experiences of any kind with persons of the opposite sex are no longer possible within the family.

When children have had mixed feelings about the family members they lost, when they had not only loved them but had also feared or hated them (often with good reason), the children's sense of bereavement is aggravated by guilt feelings. Those feelings are an additional handicap in working through and eventually overcoming the effects of such losses. Losses of family members and guilt feelings over those losses may retard the psychological development of children. Their wishes and interests differentiate more slowly. Their knowledge of the world and other people may remain fragmentary. Some things are not for them, children may fearfully feel. The ability to cooperate with others and to postpone fulfilling their goals on behalf of others may remain underdeveloped. Their motivation to work and to endure difficult tasks while postponing personal interests is not growing as might be expected; it may even decline. Pervasive changes in the environment (like war or economic crises) or strokes of fate within the family (like financial difficulties or handicapped siblings) cannot be coped with as well as in other families.

Different family members may suffer from such conflicts and losses to different degrees. The youngest usually suffer the most, unless an older or more mature family member takes it upon himself to act as a buffer. The greater a family member's subjective suffering, the more dependent on the family he becomes. The process of becoming autonomous and ready to leave the family will be impeded. Sometimes other family members seem to have a vested interest in a person's continuing dependence on the family. They may seek to overcome their own anxieties and aggressions by taking charge of and protecting another member. They need the weak member to assure themselves of their own strength and independence.

Sometimes the entire family may remain in an infantile and unstable state of mutual dependence. Bowen speaks of an *undifferentiated ego-mass* in which the family members do not have their own individualities. Their emotions are immediately contagious; they respond to each other diffusely and inarticulately (Bowen 1959, 1978, Lidz et al. 1965; also Wynne et al. 1960).

Disturbances in Family Development

Let us try to survey the pathology of family life, particularly when conflicts between and losses of family members may have caused it. In order to do that, we should consider, among other factors, the level of psychological development of individual family members and the maturity level of family life reached at the time (Bowen 1978).

Individual family members may vary in the maturity, competence, and capacity for understanding that they exhibit in relationships with other family members and with people outside the family, all of course in relation to their age. This makes for weak, average, and strong family members who participate in family life in different ways:

□ as dependent problem children in frequent or steady need of help,

□ as reliable and reasonably cooperative members who help as well as demand, if need be,

□ as leading and responsible members, sometimes also as domineering and willful persons who can do as they please in the family.

In their activities and relationships outside the family they are, respectively,

□ weak, slow, or passive and not very successful,

□ adequately active, versatile, and on the whole successful,

□ very efficient, active, self-assured and quite successful.

If a family member's developmental level outside the family differs from that within the family, the family is

inclined to ignore the discrepancy at first. When the difference persists—when, for instance, a person is continually
more mature outside the family than within—his status in
the family may improve. Inversely, a person could be strong
in the family, but may have failed repeatedly and decisively
outside the family. His status in the family may be weakened.

The maturity level of family life itself depends on the
communication habits of its members. The children's communications concern only family life at first, but to the extent
of time spent outside the home, their activities, experiences,
and adventures on the playground, in the street, in school,
in a children's or youth group, at sports, etc., are also
reported and discussed. In turn, the children begin to get
interested in the parents' activities and experiences outside
the family.

A moderately mature family life enables its members to
discuss at least their most important experiences and events
and to find sympathetic ears, but it also demands that they
themselves listen. If they only scream or if they are unre-
sponsive, family life may be below average. It need not be
that way, however. In some families mutual understanding
is good without a great many words, and screaming per se is
not yet a sure sign that there is hatred. Some families are
merely ruder than others.

When family members speak freely with each other
about all that moves them, family life can be on a high
maturity level. It can also be that a compulsion prevails
among them to have no secrets, to adhere strictly to the
family's mores and customs, not to admit friends and
acquaintances (or anybody, for that matter) to their family
life, and to forbid their members to join other families,
groups, or social contexts.

The maturity level of family life may change with time
and with the development of the children. Among the many

deviations in family development, delays and different rates of growth among family members are of general importance.

Delays in Family Development

Delays in family development may mean nothing more than children leave the family later than expected or not at all. When they leave, belatedly, they may not find partners of their own or found a family. It has been mentioned before that academic careers tend to produce such delays. A more severe form of developmental impairment would be the breakup of a family before the children are ready to leave. Although they are not yet independent personalities, the family within which they have grown up and been socialized no longer exists. Sometimes losses of one or both parents are the reason for the breakup. Occasionally a family may remain overtly intact, their home maintained and all members residing together, but communication among them has ceased. They live like strangers alongside each other.

More frequently a family breakup accompanies a loss of the family home or of its accessibility to some of the members, perhaps for geographic or psychological reasons, such as being deeply hurt or cross. The worst situation is when children no longer meet at the parents', the remaining parents', or substitute parents' home, and when they have also lost contact with each other. One could call such a course of events a break in family development. Usually, however, an impairment of development has preceded it. The scattered family members had not reached adequate maturity, autonomy, intellectual or vocational competence, or social skill before the breakup occurred. They can now learn no more about family life. Some of the scattered members may find substitute persons and groups, even substitute families whom they can join. When such families do not merely keep them until the crisis of a breakup is over but let them stay, personality development may resume in the new context.

Less fortunate members of such broken families may not find the courage to enter new personal relationships or start families of their own. If they do start a family after all, the prognosis for that family will not be good. What they themselves have been through is hard to hide from their partners and children. Unnoticed at first but insidious in effect, the pain of the old breakup infiltrates their new family life. An exception may be when marriage partners have worked on that trauma beforehand and have had the help of friends or psychotherapists.

There are other forms of impaired development in which only individual family members or subgroups of the family may be involved. Mother and daughter may, for example, enter a sadly romantic symbiosis of disappointed souls, perhaps crying to each other about callous or indifferent men, whereas Father and sons are able to assert themselves and the sons can leave the family. Or parents hold back one of their two daughters in the family and try to expel the other.

Regardless of the kind of declines in their development, families may arrest at various levels the personality development of one or more of their children and prolong the forms of social relationship and interaction typical of those levels well beyond their proper times. Children may be expected to remain in puberty, for instance, so that they may dream of ideal love relationships but are expected to refrain from love in reality. Or they may indulge in love relationships, but the parents finance them so that the children will not leave home. A particularly traumatic experience for a child or young person would be an incestuous relationship.

Even a latent love bond to a parent or a sibling in adolescence or adulthood may represent a prolongation of the oedipal phase or an arrest in that phase. In such cases, emotional ties among family members as well as those between the children and people outside the family are likely to be confused and unstable. There are endless misunderstandings and misrepresentations.

In some families love may be prohibited altogether; only work is allowed. Everyone is supposed to accomplish phenomenal things. Family members compete with each other for excellence, wanting to become the greatest of all families or rather to have the best of all individuals gloriously assembled in the family, even when there is otherwise little fun or closeness within the family. It could be that power, influence, prestige, and security, rather than achievement and work are the beacons of family life. The person wielding the greatest amount of control over others or boasting of the largest following is then the "winner."

The severest obstruction to personality development would be the perpetuation of the passivity phase in early childhood. When a family's offspring can neither make the effort to work, to achieve, and to fight for security nor to court and love but wish only to placidly doze along, expecting to be loved and taken care of, the prognosis for a happy and productive life may be extremely poor. In such a family at least one member must be different from the rest. Otherwise the family would perish. That member must provide the family with food, entertainment, and recreation — perhaps even servants. He or she is usually the only or primary breadwinner.

Such a regressive state of family life is often created or caused by a parent who is a passive personality. He or she needs an interminable and unconditional supply of motherly love. If he can't get it, he tends to become sick and pampered, a drunkard or depressed. If Father is the sick person, Mother will have to hold things together in the family. If Mother is the sick one, Father will have to do it. If both parents are sick, another family member, grandmother, aunt, uncle, or perhaps state or local welfare organization will have to take care of the family. In that case, however, the family may disintegrate before long.

Incomplete families or families who have lost a parent are in increased need of support and help. They regress more frequently than intact families do to earlier levels of family life, to a state of disinterest in work and in love, ultimately even to the level of complete passivity.

Families that have never been intact, particularly father-less households with children stemming from several different fathers, have exceptionally poor prospects. The poorest of them all are children who have grown up in children's homes or in public institutions that do not even attempt to simulate family lives. In permanently incomplete families that often need outside help in order to survive at all, the danger of grave deterioration in family development and of its members running away from home is substantial. Another danger is that run-away family members will probably not be able to generate a family of their own or, if they do, it will be only in the image of their incomplete families of origin.

Psychological and psychotherapeutic observers claim that illegitimate births and fatherless or parentless households are heritable—a piece of black humor, apparently, that is substantiated by many tragic patterns of life observable among people coming from such sad family configurations. They propagate their kind. It appears that one of the most basic conditions of a happy family life is the spouses' sincere wish to have children. Sincerity of that wish implies that the prospective parents know how, by their own wits and means, to provide for their children. Otherwise, in the best interest of the children, they should not even aspire to have them. That is what experienced clinical observers tend to recommend.

Different Rates of Growth in Individual and Family Development

Rapid development would be as good or better than average development of family life provided all family members are included in comparable ways and no significant areas of family life are impaired in the process. A weaker family member than the others, an asthenic or a less intelligent child, may be unable to keep pace with such rapid growth. In fact, he may fall farther and farther behind his siblings and the level of family life as a whole. More than in an average family, he may become the black sheep of the family and their burden. However, that is after all a family plight, unless they take special measures to reintegrate that member somehow into family life.

When rapid family development is due to special achievements of all family members or to the attention and publicity they get because of, say, the high office or the great popularity of one or both parents, disadvantages of a special kind may result. Because of the pace of whatever common life exists in the family, the members' needs for relaxation and recreation as well as for emotional understanding and personal attention may be neglected. In spite of the parents' efforts to the contrary, the children may feel left out and unhappy. If the family has a considerable public life, the children may not get to see their parents as they really are. Moreover, the children may not be permitted to become the persons that they want to be and develop those interests that are truly dear to them.

If there are none of these disadvantages, there would be no psychological objections to an accelerated development of family life. Even delays in progress would, in fact, be psychologically unobjectionable as long as the family's social environment could tolerate the lapse in growth and grant the family member's more time. If possible, everyone should be able to choose his or her own pace. A slow-growing or less mature family may indeed be excused by people around them, perhaps for their artistic merits, for their charming naiveté, or their ever-pleasant disposition. Their extravagances or failures may not be considered as offensive as they would in ordinary families and may even diminish in time. Such a family, too, continues to develop.

More often, however, the social environment, particularly the relatives, neighbors, the community, and colleagues may well feel overtaxed by the extra tolerance that is demanded of them. They wonder why that family is treated better than any others or have an easier life or be permitted to act less maturely than everyone else?

It may be hard to blame the persons in the social environment for such limits to their patience. Even in their own families, tolerance and forgiveness for weaker family members is rarely generous. Within their families, too, the weaker members need more time to grow than others. They tend to reach a given level of personality development and social life only later. Yet who should put up with such slow-paced growth and delayed achievement of given educational goals other than the parents and siblings of the person concerned? Neighbors, colleagues, and the community as a whole are necessarily not as caring of that person as is the family itself.

===4===

FAMILY THERAPY
IN
PRACTICE

As we have outlined in Chapter 3 family therapists of all varieties have similar ideas about family development and its disturbances. They consider growing up in a family the optimum place for the individual to develop but that conflicts among family members, particularly in childhood and youth, represent serious disruptions of personality development. They are familiar with the types of growth disruptions that have been described, and a few others. They usually consider a diagnosis of the family situation a prerequisite for the proper treatment of the family. Diagnostic sources about a family range from data given by the referring institution, from questionnaires prepared by therapists that one or more members of the family are asked to fill out (either before the first session or later on) to trial sessions with the family. During these sessions the therapist should clarify the extent to which family therapy will be offered.

The family's composition of persons is usually considered an indispensable diagnostic feature regardless of whether the entire family is coming or merely an emissary. This data should include: age and sex of children and age of parents, if possible, age and sex of parents' siblings, their marital status and respective number of children. It is also essential to obtain information about whether the parents' parents are still alive or lost through death or divorce and when in the lives of the parents those losses occurred. Losses suffered by the client family themselves (whether of children or parents), substitution of losses (e.g., a stepfather, an aunt, or a grandmother), or the entry of new persons into the family (e.g., stepsiblings or half-siblings) should also be recorded. Of further importance are the school and vocational careers of family members, the changes of family residence, and the illnesses, especially those that necessitated separations of family members. A family member (including the patients' parents) living apart from the family and the distance of that member's residence from the family site should be noted as well.

Even when a family therapist uses no questionnaire or guidesheet about how to collect information during an interview, he almost can't help collecting all the data anyway in a carefully conducted interview with at most occasional inquiries regarding incomplete information or clarification of apparent contradictions. With these data the family therapist is able to appraise what family members have responded to in the past and what they are, or are no longer, responding to now. He can by and large understand how family life has developed and how the life situation has come about in which the family finds itself at the beginning of treatment.

Where the data have not been collected, either by neglect or on purpose, the family therapist's diagnostic understanding of his clients and his ability to document his psychotherapeutic work may well be put in question. Evaluation of psychotherapy including family therapy is hardly possible without a record of the life situation of the patient or the family at the beginning of treatment. Only with such a record can the distance that a family has covered while in psychotherapy be recognized.

Without long-term evaluation of at least some of his clients, a family therapist's diagnostic and therapeutic understanding would be hard to attest to or improve. Only by comparing life and family situations during therapy (which was hopefully recorded) and after therapy can the family therapist learn something about the appropriateness of his or her psychotherapeutic behavior.

Arguments against the need for understanding both present and past objective life situations of patients in psychotherapy have come from nondirective or client-centered psychotherapists (e.g., Hart and Tomlinson 1970, Rogers 1951, Tausch 1968) and from behavior therapists (e.g., Bandura 1969, Eysenck and Rachman 1966, Meyer and Chesser 1970, Wolpe and Lazarus 1966, Yates 1970).

Nondirective (or client-centered) psychotherapists argue that the patients' emotional experiences and behavior are the vital issues in therapy. Moreover, they claim the factual aspects of those experiences are irrelevant, and the patients' objective life situation—both past and present—are not the *real* concerns of the psychotherapist. Anything important will be reflected in the patient's feelings. Behavior therapists claim, in turn, that only the patient's current faulty behavior is up for modification in the present and future.

Communication therapists express similar opinions (e.g., Laing et al. 1966, Watzlawick et al. 1967). They want to modify the patient's current modes of communication with his social environment. To the extent that they concern themselves with family therapy or partner therapy (e.g., Berne 1964, Harris 1967, Mandel et al. 1971, 1975), however, it is apparent that they are not all that strict in practice. Their case records reveal that there are emotional responses to the past as well as to the present, and objective life circumstances of past and present do in fact emerge in therapy. This happens to nondirective therapists too at times, and behavior therapists in the last ten years have considerably extended evaluations of their patients at the beginning of treatment. There are even approximations to classical psychotherapy.

On the other hand, compared with classical individual, child, or group psychotherapy, *family therapists* are more inclined to abandon their neutrality and their personal self-restraint in psychotherapeutic interventions. According to Ackerman (1966), Bowen (1965, 1978), Minuchin (1974), Satir (1967), and colleagues, the family therapist acts as a parent figure, an educator, and a model as well as a testing partner for new attitudes and interests of family members or the family as a whole. That is to say, he does not only recognize transference behavior in the client family, he may select, underline, and even provoke it. Moreover, the family therapist may give family members permission to speak and may occasionally interrupt them. He may instruct and offer comparisons from his clinical or even his personal experience. He may address himself to implicit or nonverbal communications in treatment. He may praise, support, or encourage at certain times and attempt to soothe the family's anxieties. Treatment benefits when the family develops a feeling of security and trust in the family therapist. When necessary, he can deepen their sense of trust by the comments and attitudes he displays.

Family therapists take other liberties, too, that classical psychotherapy would not allow. They order truant family members to come to family sessions and, when necessary, will ask family members to switch seats in the treatment room. They may ask for enactments or repetitions of fights in the family, for demonstrations of behavior discussed or remembered in the session, and for role playing or role swapping. Under certain circumstances the family therapist may even come to the family's house. Occasionally the entire therapy is conducted in the family's house.

Family therapists may see family members individually, sometimes even without prior consent from the rest of the family. Family therapists would not hide the fact of such treatments from other members, though, and may even encourage the person involved to tell the family about the content of the individual session.

Family therapists may bring co-therapists along to some or all of their sessions. Frequently the co-therapist is of the opposite sex. Sometimes both therapists may see family members individually. At other times they may have two, three, or more families for multiple family therapy.

Finally, some family therapists make audio- or video-tapes of their sessions. This requires the family's explicit consent, which they may not be willing to give, but occasionally a therapist asks for it so insistently that it would be difficult for the family to refuse the request. Some families may look at the tapes for psychotherapeutic purposes, or they may even take them home for further study.

CAN FAMILY THERAPY BE CLASSICAL PSYCHOTHERAPY?

All these interventions and practices deviate from classical psychotherapy. The majority of family therapists use them only under special conditions and are aware of the potential complications they entail for the psychotherapeutic process. Some of these interventions are daring. They may have too little empirical evidence of success to be attempted in strict classical psychotherapy at all. They may even fail. The family therapist may have acted on intuition and impulse. He may have acted in countertransference and thus aroused unrealistic expectations in the family. Perhaps he wanted to pull off a big show, to perform a miracle, possibly to impress a family member, or to outdo a parent.

The family does not ordinarily tolerate such brashness for long. They do not really believe in miracles. It could also be that they feel so awed by the superior and nonchalant air of the family therapist that they, or at least some of them, stop telling him what they really remember, feel, or mean. It may be that the family experiences the therapist as a showman or show-off and unconsciously develops an interest in having him fall flat on his face. Eventually they don't even believe his psychotherapeutic motivation. He does not merely want to help; he wants something else as well. He wants something for himself.

The temptation of showmanship and exhibitionism— the temptation to display competence, conviction, or psychotherapeutic powers—is greater with family therapists than with classical individual or child therapists. A group therapist may also be tempted in that vein, but the group of people that he has assembled who are supposedly strangers to each other are usually much more amenable to treatment than a family. The family is a closed group that does not just come together for treatment, but rather has lived together for a long time. It is hard for the family therapist to get a foot in the door that the family may have opened in need or even by mistake. He realizes that he must make an impression soon. He must show that he is calm and sure, that the conflicts, threats, and anxieties of the family do not scare or confuse him. He must try to clarify something in the first session that they had not realized but that they can now see. If he does not make such an impression, a family may soon lose interest in therapy. When he broaches unpleasant topics, the family may become evasive, and if he insists on raising such topics, the family may stop coming.

Many family therapists try to stick to the rules and principles of classical psychotherapy. They do not assume roles in advance nor do they instruct or educate. They tell their patients nothing about themselves or about their clinical experience with other patients. They only take up themes that the family or any member of the family has already mentioned, whether intentionally or not. Family therapists are neutral and caring in their interest in all that the family wants to say or has expressed in the past, but they do not praise, encourage, or admonish if they can help it. They try to get the whole family to treatment or merely both parents, as the case may be, but they do not insist that all come or that they come every time. Many family therapists do not see any family members individually as long as family therapy is going on. They do not see the family in the family's own house.

Sometimes they do take audio- or videotapes of the family sessions, but they do not let the family take them home. They usually refrain from demonstrating the tapes in family therapy sessions. If they do show them, they prefer to do so with all family members present and to give them ample opportunity to talk about what they have watched and heard.

Whatever the family produces together in terms of communications, memories, thoughts, fantasies, feelings, opinions, and conflicts is the material of treatment in family therapy. The family therapist should not provide or admit information from other sources in his psychotherapeutic interventions. In fact, he should not even have other sources. He should use only information which the family members know that he has. They were present when he was told; they were witnesses. That is why the classical family therapist tries to avoid individual sessions with members of the family once family therapy has started. That is also why he does not accept written messages, letters, diaries, or essays from individual members. He could take up such material in family therapy only if all members were familiar with it, and then he would actually have to verify what they still remember of it.

Acceptance of any written material, even one coming from the family as a whole, would cost the family therapist extra time and, once accepted, be considered a precedent for more written correspondence with the therapist. The same would hold for a family member trying to telephone the therapist outside of therapy sessions.

In individual as well as family therapy, the classical psychotherapist's answer to such extracurricular contact attempts is friendly nonacceptance of the written message and the assurance that its subject can be discussed in the next therapeutic session. The patient should broach the issue then and talk about it.

The more strictly family therapists adhere to the classical form of psychotherapy, the more likely it is that patients hesitate at first with their inner commitment to the treatment. When they eventually do catch on, however, their work tends to be more serious and steady. They get more out of it, and whatever therapeutic success they reach seems to be more independent of the psychotherapist's personality. The classical family therapist helps the family to help itself. The deviant psychotherapist, especially the charismatic and idiosyncratic psychotherapist, helps the patient, but he goes beyond classical treatment. He takes part in the daily life of his patient or of the client family. He may invite families to his team conferences and scientific conventions and have them tell the audience how they liked his family therapy. He does not only help his patients, but he also wants them to help him. Patients should get well for the sake of the therapist. They should add another laurel to his wreath of therapeutic successes.

Classical psychotherapists are vain too, but they resist

their vanity more persistently. They do not really want publicity, whereas the charismatic, the characters or mavericks among psychotherapists, particularly in group and family therapy, love the limelight. They forget that their appearance in public actually disqualifies them among those patients who have gotten to know them there. At the least, such therapists are making psychotherapy more difficult and complicated for their patients. The patients know too much about their psychotherapist, no matter how incomplete the public image of the psychotherapist may actually be. It would be best for the patients to know nothing at all about their psychotherapist and during treatment to learn nothing about him as a person. They should rather learn to deal better with their own feelings, motives, and conflicts the way their psychotherapist (a well-meaning but neutral observer, not implicated in the patient's daily life) would see and handle their problems. Ideally they will eventually be able to do it themselves.

THE EFFECTS OF FAMILY THERAPY

One could argue that it does not matter whether classical, or less traditional, or even charismatic family therapy is being offered. What matters are the therapeutic successes.

There is little one can say against that. Success speaks for itself. It is not so easy, however, to test psychotherapeutic success. Continuation of family life in the treated family, the psychological normality of the children in school, on the job, and in their social contacts, ultimately the children's ability one day to found their own families and raise children who are psychologically normal in turn—all these are among the minimal criteria of psychotherapeutic success. In order to learn whether these criteria apply, however, one would have to wait for quite a while and keep track of all family members that had been in treatment. Psychotherapists rarely attempt to do that and rarely succeed.

In the majority of cases psychotherapists have to be content with evaluations of treatment right at the end of it. Such an appraisal more resembles a prognosis than an evaluation, even more so when the psychotherapist does it himself. The patients are only just beginning to test the insights and inner changes in their daily life that they have experienced in psychotherapy. Whether they can indeed relax more easily, work, fight, cooperate, and negotiate with others better, or pursue their love interests more vigorously and realistically than before, remains to be seen.

Paradoxically the classical psychotherapist is at a certain disadvantage in this respect compared with the charismatic psychotherapist. The classical psychotherapist has helped the patient, the group of patients, or the family to help themselves. Provided their life situations do not radically deteriorate, they should need no more psychotherapy. When treatment was terminated, this was a farewell to, or an inner separation from, the psychotherapist, facilitated by identification with the psychotherapist and with his ways of dealing with the patients' problems. If you like, the patients are taking back home with them those forms of intervention that the psychotherapist used frequently or insistently. Even in the absence of the therapist they can still resort to them in times of need. Yet they have not taken him home in their minds as a person. They only utilize his anonymous psychotherapeutic or interactional skills. The psychotherapist has really let them go. This is how many patients experience it.

In family therapy this means, among other things, that the family members are now relating to each other in the style of their (former) family therapist and his relationships to them. This style may even hold up in new critical periods. The family members listen to each other. They let others finish talking so that everyone has his say. They even try to check and confirm at times what they think they heard another say. Such a manner of relating would attest to something like minimal success in family therapy. It can be accomplished in most cases often after fairly short periods of treatment. It can be attained even in those families in which a deeper understanding of their problems and the willingness to change their family life were not yet apparent.

The charismatic psychotherapist, the "healer by surprise and magic" usually does not let his patients leave at the end of treatment. This is how the patient sees it and how he behaves. Yet many of those miracle men or women are more indifferent to and ignorant of the patient than he imagines. They soon forget him, even though the patient is carrying a burdensome piece of his psychotherapist in him. He believes in his therapist, and his improvement or cure is tied to this faith. If this faith were shaken, however, his mental state would be in jeopardy again.

Such patients are inclined to stay emotionally bound to the therapist for a long time or for life and to keep trying to communicate with him. The charismatic psychotherapist, in turn, would have to respond to this, at least in some form, possibly with a printed handout, if he does not want to endanger that patient's psychotherapeutic cure.

Classical psychotherapists call this a *transference cure*. The psychotherapist has not only observed and tolerated the fact that at times during treatment he assumed different roles in the patient's mind (those of a father, a teacher, a mother, a big sister, a friend, a tormentor, etc.), but has actively adopted such roles himself, that is, that of the renowned, powerful, happy, and indulgent father or say that of the irresistible prophet of a great love movement. In this he has made radical selections from among the patients' various transference tendencies. Many of those tendencies were never admitted by him in therapy, whereas a few others were forced upon the patients, such as the wish to entrust themselves unconditionally in childlike humility, to the great guru and to be content with mere crumbs of his favor. To get to the point, it is almost inherent in such circumstances that the charismatic psychotherapist who is in effect less interested in his patients than he is in himself and his miracles, may get more spontaneous feedback from his patients than the classical psychotherapist. The latter should not get any spontaneous feedback if he has truly helped his patients.

The psychotherapist who does not operate on the basis of charisma and blind trust, but deviates from classical psychotherapy in that, sooner or later, he finally resorts to acting as counselor, educator, teacher, or coach may, after all, have his therapeutic successes, too. If they last, there can hardly be objections. Yet such successes usually are not as transparent or as well-understood. The patient may be given the routine treatment, a program that this counseling or managing psychotherapist may have planned in advance, either in toto or in parts. He is providing ready-made goods. He often cannot distinguish the various effects they produce on different patients. His treatment may be shorter, though, than other treatments. The classical psychotherapist, in contrast, is offering his goods tailor-made. He heeds all aspects that a patient or family presents and usually understands much more accurately what is going on in psychotherapy.

INDICATIONS FOR FAMILY THERAPY

As to the scope of family therapy there are different opinions, not only among psychotherapists in general, but also among family therapists. Many classical psychotherapists seem to believe today that individual therapy is always family therapy, too. In the course of treatment the patient has to clarify his relationships with his family of origin. Moreover, his relationships with love or marriage partners, or even with his own children, are another important theme of his psychotherapeutic work. Actual treatment of other family members, however, would be indicated only when the individual patients are children or adolescents themselves, still living in the family. With other age ranges individual therapy may be enough. The patient can usually handle necessary rearrangements and new understandings with his family himself.

In contrast, some family therapists think that any psychological disturbance can only be cured by actually treating the entire family (see e.g., Ackerman 1966, Bowen 1965, 1978, Minuchin 1974). This is particularly true of psychoses. The majority of family therapists, however, are more eclectic and pragmatic. Certain school problems of children, work- and prestige-related conflicts of adults, problems of unmarried adults with their lovers, their studies, or their first down-to-earth work experiences usually need no family or partner therapy. Individual therapy will do.

Family therapy has become necessary when at least one other person in the family seems to be implicated. Family therapy is indicated for parents who cannot cope with their children, for adults who live with their parents or who have to work with them and are unhappy about it, for love and marriage partners who are not getting along with each other but do not want to separate, and for parents who do want to part but are worried about the consequences, or the distress they may inflict on their children. It should be noted that separating as friends or by mutual agreement may represent psychotherapeutic success as compared with separating in hatred, especially when there are children. Finally, family therapy can be useful for patients with special problems, such as excessive drinking on the part of a parent, the presence of a handicapped or psychotic child in the family, a working mother, or grandparents, aunts, pets, or subtenants who live with the family and cause strife and discontent in family life.

Some family therapists (e.g., Bowen 1978) deem family therapy possible and useful even with only a single member. The patient is partly working through his family problems with family members at home. If requested, other family members may join the patient's treatment. Like all members of group or family therapy who are joining at a later stage, they may be at a disadvantage and, accordingly, insecure or distrustful. For people and families with little education, for members of the lower class, or of marginal groups in the population, family therapy may be indicated when they have domestic or personal problems. Often such persons are not used to talking about themselves and their relationships with others. Individual therapy, therefore, may not be to their liking, but in family therapy their communications are often more sincere, courageous, and spontaneous than in other groups of the population (see e.g., Minuchin 1974, Richter 1970).

THE FAMILY THERAPIST

If a psychotherapist does not have a certain need to prove himself in this most difficult of all psychotherapeutic disciplines, if he does not enjoy the higher risks, the complexity, and the turbulence that occur during treatment, he would probably never have become a family therapist. Individual therapy would surely have been safer and more comfortable. If family therapy is successful, however, its efficacy, as a rule, is greater than that of individual therapy. The family therapist is trying to understand the relationships between the parents, between the parents and children, and between the children themselves. If he succeeds, parents and children can benefit. In fact, successful family therapy may continue to influence the expectations and interests of the children when they have grown up and are founding their own families. Even the overall mood in these families may have been set at least to some extent by the family therapy that transpired twenty or more years earlier.

A would-be family therapist may be striving for that greater efficacy and may want to use his time better than he can in individual therapy. He wants to be more socially effective than the classical therapist, particularly the psychoanalyst. He can achieve this goal, however, only at the expense of a certain precision in his work and understanding.

At scientific conferences of family therapists, one is impressed by the number of demonstrations of family therapy that utilize audio- and videotapes. What surprises one is how little the reporting family therapist can often add to these demonstrations. The idiosyncrasies of family therapists seem to vary more widely than the demonstrated clientele or the techniques of treatment. This may have to do with the fact that the family therapist tends to pick those families for demonstrations with whom he felt most comfortable and comparatively most successful. It indicates, however, that reporting and demonstrating what one does in this complex process of family therapy is obviously more paramount at such conferences than is the theoretical understanding of the problems the family presented or the reasons for a particular course of treatment.

The scientific publications on family therapy, especially the handbooks and joint publications (e.g., Boszormenyi-Nagy and Framo 1965, Papp 1977, Richter et al. 1976) are not hiding this state of affairs. Family therapy is not old yet, and it is developing along several tracks. Given the many different personalities among family therapists and the many versions of family therapy, nobody seems to know for sure what basic, reliable, and teachable form it will ultimately take. I suppose, though, that it will remain close to classical psychotherapy and retain its roots there throughout its variations.

A person wishing to become a psychotherapist may be assumed to have had his own share of psychological problems in life and in his family. Indeed these problems are likely to have exceeded in gravity those found in the population at large. On the other hand, they have not been so grave that they would impair or disqualify him for his work as a psychotherapist. Usually he was able to cope with or even solve his problems. This is precisely necessary, to be sure, if he wants to do psychotherapy. His perceptions of the patient and his objectivity must not be impaired by his own unresolved inner problems.

A comparatively good guarantee that a future psychotherapist has resolved his own problems—to the extent that they will no longer disturb him in treating the psychological problems and conflicts of his patients—is to have successfully completed his own psychotherapy. This is required by practically all schools of classical psychotherapy of their candidates. Other schools of psychotherapy are not as rigorous. In some schools, like behavior therapy and some camps of child, group, and family therapy, the apprentices begin their psychotherapeutic work under the supervision of a training therapist, but without having undergone psychotherapy themselves.

Schools of psychotherapy differ also in the length of psychotherapeutic work they require under the supervision of training therapists and in the care they apply. Psychoanalytic institutes are said to be the most demanding. Ordinarily they require two years of psychotherapeutic work under individual and group supervision, with at least two, and often three patients. Group supervision is provided in sessions conducted by a group supervisor with several candidates in training, who take turns reporting on their work while the group supervisor and the other candidates listen, comment, and discuss.

In supervision conducted with at least two supervisors, the candidate is essentially learning to control his tendencies of countertransference, that is, his susceptibility to misperceptions and misinterpretations of the patient's utterances and behavior, and to the temptations of acting other than psychotherapeutically (e.g., giving the patient advice, information, or orders). Perfect control can hardly ever be reached, though. Even very experienced psychotherapists cannot always avoid such tendencies of countertransference, but they usually recognize them in time—that is, before they intervene therapeutically. Candidates in training commit such errors more frequently at first, but in the course of their apprenticeship these errors become progressively rarer.

This apprenticeship, psychotherapeutic work under individual and group supervision, is considered the most important part of one's training as a psychotherapist. Some claim, however, that shorter psychotherapeutic treatments under supervision with a greater number of patients (i.e., more than merely two or three) would be even more instructive.

Training as a family therapist, like that of a group therapist, should start only after the candidate has finished his own individual therapy. Most individual therapists and some family therapists agree on this. If a candidate in training has not had his own individual therapy nor practiced individual therapy for a fairly long time, he cannot keep track of the still more complicated processes involved in group and family therapy.

Other family therapists (e.g., Ackerman 1966, Bowen 1965, Richter 1970, Richter et al. 1976, Satir 1967) more or less advocate a separate course of training for family therapists. It should start, they say, with the candidate's own family therapy or with the analysis of his own family background as a kind of homework. It should be continued with the trainee's observing other family therapy via written records, audio- and videotapes, and one-way observation screens, followed by his attending family therapy sessions in person as an observer and later as a co-therapist, and ending with his own practice of family therapy—under supervision, at first, and later on his own, preferably with continuing reporting, at longer intervals, to a supervisor or team of which he is a member. Whether a candidate should also have his own individual therapy will become apparent in this process and could in certain cases be made a condition of his further training in family therapy.

There are practicing family therapists of both camps who can manage their work, who enjoy it, and who seem able to help their family patients. Often they have been exposed to the other kind of training, too. Family therapists who began immediately with family therapy have sought further training in individual therapy including their own. Family therapists who have come from individual therapy have done their own family therapy or their work with family members thereafter.

What has appeared to be of great importance with both groups of family therapists is the continuation of reporting beyond their apprenticeship, that is, their therapeutic work under supervision, in regular team conferences, with enough time for discussion and debate. Reporting includes discussing the life situation and main problems of the family in treatment, the course of treatment along with short- and medium-term evaluation of its effects.

Short-term evaluation of the effects of therapy concern the therapist's interventions, particularly his interpretations of the affects, motives, and conflicts of patients within each session. Were they appropriate? Could the patients accept them? What affective and motivational changes, what insights, what plans or resolutions did they generate (or might they have generated)?

Medium-term evaluation investigates the effects of early therapy sessions on recent ones and the changes in the patients and in their relationships to each other observable in treatment or, indirectly, in the client family's daily life. Often the reporting therapist or other members of the psychotherapy team are trying to predict how the patients and their treatment are likely to develop. The further course of treatment can confirm or invalidate such predictions.

In this manner the family therapist receives counsel and help with the treatment of at least his more difficult cases. The mere necessity of reporting explicitly, coherently, and intelligibly to his team tends to clarify his observations and interventions more than solitary and implicit reviewing alone could do. In order to report to others the therapist must keep some kind of record of the sessions; not so much audio- or videotapes as his own written notes made during or after each session. They afford him easy access to any aspect of the treatment so far. Audio- or videotapes made as records would have to be played over again by the therapist to serve their purpose. That, however, would be far too time-consuming in the daily practice of psychotherapy. In order to transform the tapes into a handy and accessible record, the therapist would have to listen to or watch the tapes and make notes. In other words, he would do in double time what other therapists did during the therapeutic sessions or immediately after. Experienced psychotherapists tend to need about ten minutes of note-taking for a fifty minute session, fifteen or twenty minutes for a ninety-minute session, as is more customary in family therapy.

Long-term evaluation—verifying the effects of psychotherapy half a year, a year, two years or more after treatment has ended—comes up in team conferences only sporadically. Often no checking of effects was possible over that length of

time. Such monitoring cannot influence the course of treatment as directly as short- or medium-term evaluations can,
anyway, unless the client family returns for more treatment.
The practice is or should be for all psychotherapy clinics and
centers to attempt long-term evaluation in some form or
other—not only with those cases who return to therapy and
may by definition represent less than successful treatment
but for all patients they have had. Systematic efforts, such as
follow-up questionnaires and discussions in the team of
available follow-up data are clearly desirable.

One of the preconditions of psychotherapy is the age of
the therapist; this holds even more for family therapy. A
person under 30 often impresses the clients and patients as
insufficiently trustworthy. In child therapy, a psychotherapist may be younger and still trustworthy for the child, but
not for the child's parents. Yet work with parents is practically indispensable in child therapy. Partner therapy for
young unmarried patients necessitates psychotherapeutic
work on the partners' relationships to their parents and
families of origin, and for that work, too, the psychotherapist
is more acceptable to patients when he or she is a bit older
than they are. Being of adequate age is even more important
for the treatment of parents and their children. Parents are
inclined to show some resistance to a therapist who, judging
by his age, is unlikely to have children or does not seem to
have them. Patients distrust such seeming inexperience; it
cannot be enough, they feel. When the therapist has reached
a certain age, however, this resistance dwindles even when
the therapist in fact has no children of his own.

Another precondition for working as a psychotherapist
is an orderly and comparatively stable life situation. The
psychotherapist should have not only understood his inner
problems and conflicts before he became a therapist but,
whenever possible, have also resolved them. Otherwise he
may not be sufficiently free and objective in his perception of
the patients' behavior, emotions, motives, and conflicts.

Some of his patients or groups of patients might then confuse him, pressure him, or tempt him into entering a personal relationship with them outside the constraints of psychotherapy. Secure living conditions, including a permanent partnership and children, count among the proofs that a therapist has come to terms with his inner problems and conflicts. An unattached psychotherapist would automatically raise the question in a patient's mind as to why he has stayed single. Did he not want to marry, or could he not? "But how," the patient will ask, "will he be able to help me with my love problems, when he has not solved his own?"

This does not mean that the psychotherapist ought to reveal his family status to his patient. He should not tell his patient anything about himself. Yet, a married therapist will be better able to divert a patient's transference behavior, such as a sudden interest in the psychotherapist's family life more casually than a therapist who has "something to hide." He will turn this curiosity into an inquiry into the reasons for his patient's question and for the interest in learning about people's families that the patient has perhaps expressed in the past and in his everyday life. The therapist may ask: "When else (besides just now) was it important for you to learn about a person's marital status?"

All this applies even more to a family therapist. He or she must be able to empathize and identify with parents and children, with males and with females, if he wants to understand the family. Parents may be suspicious of a childless psychotherapist and may think that he understands only the children but not them. The children may figure that he does not understand them, either, because he has no children to deal with at home. If on top of this the therapist does not have a partner for life, how can he understand that the parents want, or once wanted, to live together and are now having conflicts about it?

Family therapists who are unmarried or divorced, even more so, those who advocate free love and leave their children with the abandoned parent or who do not want children are known to entangle themselves in countertransference behavior, sometimes with devastating consequences for the family in treatment. Those therapists are often partisan rather than benevolently neutral and may be quite benevolent to *some* of their patients. They perceive only part of the wishes, interests, and conflicts of family members. The other part is interspersed with the therapist's own preoccupations. Instead of doing therapy he engages in friendships or civic associations with the families in treatment or with some of their members, usually at the expense of the rest, and often to the disadvantage of the family as a whole.

Whoever does family therapy cannot very well pursue the extratherapeutic goal of abolition of the family. Basically speaking, the family therapist, through his theoretical and practical experiences in psychotherapy as well as his own life, ought to be convinced of the biological, psychological, and sociological value of the family. He may also believe life in the extended family to be better than in the typical small family of modern industrial society. In the case of incomplete families he may believe that they are better off staying together than splitting up and also that, in the case of adoptive or foster families, approximating the conditions and structure of intact families is best for the children.

Moreover, a family therapist ought to have a spontaneous interest in children, in their development, and in their emotional bonds. A crying child should concern him at least as much as an unhappy puppy or baby chimpanzee.

RULES FOR CONDUCTING FAMILY THERAPY

The rules for conducting family therapy sessions have been taken from classical psychotherapy and adjusted to treatment of a group, particularly of a family. Acting on those

rules in the practice of family therapy is an art that grows
with experience, and sticking to those rules does not guarantee that the therapist has guided the session optimally.
Violation of any of the rules, however, constitutes a departure from classical psychotherapy and, in that sense, is an
"error" (Toman 1978b).

We have seen that family therapists tend to depart from
classical psychotherapy at certain times and in certain forms.
As long as they do family *therapy*—not counseling, teaching,
or just managing family life—most of them are likely to
adhere to the rules at least at the beginning of a session or
through several sessions at the beginning of longer treatment. Only then, if at all, do they depart from classical
psychotherapy and resort to non- or quasi-psychothera-
peutic interventions.

We shall not concern ourselves much with the negotiations between the family therapist or his secretary and at
least one family member that ordinarily precede the first
family session. Arranging seats, choosing play material (if
children are coming along), lighting, and possible audio- or
videotaping has also been taken care of. Information about
the need to keep dates and be on time, about the possibilities
and consequences of canceling sessions, about payment (or,
in case the family does not pay, about the agency carrying
the costs), has all been given to the client family. Perhaps an
advance agreement has been made specifying that the family
cannot casually stop therapy. Rather, such an intention has
to be expressed beforehand so that the desire to end therapy
can be discussed during the rest of the session or in still
another session or two, just as the family therapist himself
would do if he suggested termination of treatment.

Let us now consider the rules for conducting family
therapy.

1.   The family therapist listens attentively in an attitude of
benevolent neutrality. All family members should be able to

say whatever comes to mind. All should be permitted to finish what they want to say and should try to listen when the others are talking. If necessary, the family therapist will explicitly instruct the family that these are the guidelines he suggests and will try to follow himself.

2.   The family therapist lets the family choose the topics. Family members may say what occurs to them or what is on their minds. Organizational or practical questions regarding the treatment situation are an exception as is the course of treatment. The therapist does not tell anything about himself and does not help the family or any of its members concretely or materially. He does help the family, though, to pursue their topics and to unfold them. He encourages family members to give examples of what they mean. The family members may instruct or inform each other and talk about themselves. Outside of the treatment sessions they are free to do as they please.

3.   The family therapist himself only takes up topics which the family has already broached in the current session. He tries to do so when there are pauses in the family discourse and he must heed the following subrules:

a. Among several possible topics the family therapist chooses that which dates farther back in the family's past (or in the family sessions held so far). When the family has been sticking to topics in the past, however, he may choose a more recent one instead. When, for instance, one of two birthday parties mentioned occurred several years ago, and the other several weeks ago, the therapist will rather be interested in the first one.

b. Among several possible topics the family therapist chooses that which aroused affect in the family or at least in one family member, or one that did not seem to but, in fact, should have by its content. One of the children may, for example, turn silent after having joined the family in describing their very beautiful summer vacation a year ago. When the therapist asked about his silence, the child related that in the subsequent fall he had to repeat his class in school, whereas his best friend had been promoted. The friendship weakened thereafter.

c. Among several possible topics, the family therapist chooses that in which external or internal conflicts of the family become apparent. They may be conflicts in the family's past or present, conflicts of daily life, or conflicts occurring in the treatment sessions. Mother may, for instance, admit that the beautiful summer vacations mentioned above were not so beautiful for her. As it turns out upon inquiry, they had rented a house in which she had to do all the housework. Father was of no help at all, but was flirting instead with another summer guest.

d. When affects or conflicts in the family or on the part of one of its members are directed at the family therapist who himself has not, to his knowledge, provoked such affects or conflicts, the family therapist suggests that the family or the family member search for similar affects or conflicts in their past or present daily life. This suggestion may be preceded by a question as to what in the treatment situation may have aroused the affect or conflict. Father may claim, for example, that the family therapist, a woman, has taken sides with his wife and daughter. Questioned as to the basis for this judgment, father replies that the therapist had ignored his point of view (that there should be equal rights and responsibilities for all; that girls are not princesses and should get their hands dirty. As it happened, the therapist had given the family this very interpretation of the father's feelings toward the girls, however, without expressing herself as pro or con). When else has Father or the family had the impression that a man's position has been disregarded, the therapist might ask next; or, when else have they felt that a person was collaborating with the women against the men?

Rule (d) obviously concerns the handling of the patients' transference behavior by the therapist. Yet, in a group, unprovoked affects and conflicts may be directed not only at the therapist, but also at other group members. Group members show transference behavior also toward each other. In such instances, the family therapist may intervene in a similar fashion. He may suggest that the group explore the possible causes of those affects and conflicts and inquire whether they had ever before experienced such reactions and conflicts. There is a difference, though. In contrast to the therapist the group or family members are not obliged to respond to transference behavior of other group or family members in a psychotherapeutic manner. Ordinarily, they do rather the opposite. They respond to affects and conflicts directed at them with feelings of their own. They defend themselves. They counterattack or knuckle under. The therapist, as the benevolently neutral observer, has a hard time, however, distinguishing between family members' imagined wrongs and reality or catching the beginning of such an interaction, in which one word leads to the other. There are dangers for the therapist of countertransference behavior—that is, of a priori opinions and arbitrary sympathies.

In family therapy there is an additional complication as compared with group therapy: some transferences by one family member onto another have not only occurred in the treatment session, but were going on long before treatment even began. They may be called long-term transferences. They are chronic misunderstandings of another person in the light of one's own wishes and past experiences.

A mother may believe, for example, that her children are exploiting her and refusing to grow up and that their father is supporting them in this behavior. (She had been with foster parents herself for several years in her childhood, had returned to her parents only when she started school, and had later on been sent to a boarding school at the wish of her father so that "her altruism and independence would be encouraged.") Or, say, a child believes that she is the least favored child in the family. (As the middle sister of an older brother and a younger sister, she was shocked when her younger sister arrived and thereafter felt too little loved by her parents and her brother. She interprets even the slightest neglect of her wishes as confirmation of that situation.) Or a father worries that his son may grow into an aggressive, evil human being. (Father himself had to put up with a strict father, was never allowed to object, and lost him in his youth through an avalanche that killed his father but spared him.) Such long-term or chronic transferences among family members may have to be traced to past family life, not merely into the current or preceding treatment sessions in which they came up. What's more, the examples of similar behavior in the past and in the daily life of the family to which the family therapist may (and ought to) direct the discussion may precipitate new controversies. Family members may not remember some of the events or conflicts mentioned or may remember them in a quite different way from the reporting family member.

4.   During the family discussion the family therapist tries, among other things, to explore the objective circumstances of a family's life situation, including those of the parents in their respective families of origin. Contradictory representations by different family members may have to coexist for the

time being. A version of events that all concerned could agree upon may emerge or be searched for if the event comes up again.

While obtaining information about those objective circumstances of life, the other rules of conducting family therapy are not abandoned. The family therapist may probe further, but when the family digresses, he will allow the digression and may sometimes have to wait a long time before getting back to the events in question. Occasionally an objective detail may remain unclarified throughout the treatment. The family therapist permits all family members to inquire into such objective circumstances of family life. Family members, in contrast to the therapist, may persist in trying to clarify something. This is acceptable as long as family members can speak freely and without interruption.

5.   As in individual or group therapy, the family therapist tries to keep the family discourse going. To that end he may ask questions, make comments, express hunches, and offer interpretations.

Interpretations are designations of affects, motives, interests, or conflicts of the family that appear to be at the root of a sequence of communications among family members in session. They may concern past or present family life or the exchanges in therapy. Interpretations usually have greater news value for the family than the therapist's comments or questions. They may surprise some family members and may sometimes frighten or annoy them, sometimes delight or depress them.

Interpretations are considered accepted, as a rule, only when all family members have accepted them. Provisionally the family therapist may be content with a majority acceptance. Arguments over the issue may go on and may stretch over several sessions. When the family wants to digress from the subject of the interpretation, the family therapist will let them. He may hope, though, that the topic will come up again or he may even attempt to bring it up himself provided he is afforded an opportunity within the constraints of the rules of family therapy.

In his interventions (comments, questions, hunches, interpretations) the family therapist strives to follow the interests and wishes of the family as a whole, but without neglecting the interests and wishes of individual family members. In the records of his sessions he is at pains to trace the course of topics. He may do this without explicit reference to individual family members. He records what "the family" said. He notes the topics they took up as a group.

6.   The family therapist tries to pursue and think through the family's topics in his own mind. He tests thematic and behavioral sequences in a family session, including his own interventions, for internal consistency and overall meaning. He does this silently throughout the session, but explicitly after the session, while jotting down his notes. What do the family members want secretly or unconsciously, as well as openly and consciously, and where do their interests clash? Such are the family therapist's silent questions. He does not concern himself only with the current session but also with the previous ones, and with the life history and life situation of the family as he has come to know it.

7.   When family members occasionally respond psychotherapeutically to other family members or to the family as a whole and when they intervene in ways that the family therapist himself would have chosen, he lets them.

8.   When, however, such an attempt by an intervening family member violates one or more rules of conducting family therapy, the family therapist waits for other family members to disapprove or to take exception. If no one does and if the family has not moved on to other themes, he intervenes in accordance with the rules of conducting family therapy.

9.　　When a family member intervenes often or regularly like a psychotherapist, the family therapist comments on and interprets the family member's behavior. He will do that even when the family member concerned intervenes appropriately and when there are no objections from other family members. Then the family may debate whether they will continue to accept this behavior in view of the fact that this family member may be exempting himself or herself from the family discussion. Do they want to have a family member to serve as an extra therapist? Has the family therapist become expendable? Is treatment over or can it be continued at home? Should all family members be permitted at times to act as therapist? Or should the family therapist become a family member? Questions like these merit discussion.

10.　　A long-term goal of family therapy is the continuation of family discussion outside the treatment sessions and after treatment has been terminated. When family members, at least occasionally, listen and make an effort to understand each other and allow each other to speak freely without interruption, a minimal goal of family therapy has already been achieved. Family members have learned to communicate better among themselves. If their responses to each other sometimes resemble those of the therapist, it may come to them as no surprise.

When they are able, moreover, to coordinate their actions better than before; when they know themselves and other family members better and learn to sense their own and the others' needs, longings, and anxieties; when they are able not only to pursue their own wishes and interests within and outside the family less fearfully and more successfully, but can also help other family members to do so; when they are having more fun together than they used to; when they can leave the family longer than ever before possible without feeling guilty and when they can return to the family without being berated; when their friendships and love relationships outside the family are not obstructed by family members, but rather understood or even encouraged; when such friends or other partners can come into the family and can count on being allowed to talk and listened to; ultimately, when the young family members generate families and friends of their own and live mostly in peace with each other—when all that is so, family therapy may well have achieved far more than minimal success.

The goals of classical psychotherapy are inherent in family therapy's goals. In classical individual therapy the patient is helped to regain opportunities for living, action, and satisfaction that he believed lost to him, especially those that are accessible to most other people. In greater detail, the goal of classical psychotherapy is the improvement of the patient's opportunities to satisfy his leisure and recreational needs, his competitive, power and/or cooperation needs, and his heterosexual love needs. The latter includes increasing a patient's capacity for intimacy and for efforts and sacrifice on behalf of the beloved as well as the capacity for patience and tolerance (see also Toman 1978a, b).

All these goals are implicit in the more modest goal of family therapy: the continuation of family discussions between treatment sessions and after treatment is over. This more modest goal enables the family therapist to try psychotherapy even with people who are reluctant to commit themselves, who have little time, who may be willing to come for only one session. When a family therapist can demonstrate to such a family not by persuasion, but by their actual experiences, that family communication is possible, that they are not losing their identities when they try family therapy, that they can continue to act in their daily lives in their customary way, that they are not being forced to do or say anything, and that they need not feel guilty when they decline an offer of more treatment (but rather may try again at a later time with the same or different therapist)—when a family therapist can accomplish only these inroads he has not acted in vain.

This is a far cry from the early ideal of classical individual psychotherapy in which all of a person's experiences and memories, all his wishes and frustrations, all the anxieties, aggressions, and depressions of his life have to be worked through before treatment can end. However, the goals of family therapy are realistic. One is reminded of the fact that even Freud wondered one day whether psychoanalysis is indeed ever terminable (Freud 1937). He recommended that psychoanalysts be content with a certain amount of psychoanalytic treatment and with limited or partial success in some cases. There is hope that such patients may continue to improve or at least stabilize themselves without further treatment or that strokes of luck may help them.

At any rate, family therapy ought to be tried wherever possible. The mental and emotional suffering that can originate in family life is of such grave consequence and families themselves are so important for the maintenance of a humane world that even the smallest degree of help will matter.

This is not to say that everybody or every family needs family therapy, even if there are very few who could not benefit from it. In many families the parents have accumulated enough experience from their families of origin and from their contacts with friends and neighbors and are enjoying their children sufficiently to engage in spontaneous family conversations. Sometimes these amount to explicit discussions. Casual conversations about all sorts of matters are usually a regular feature of family life and are carried on during meals, family evenings, weekends, or holidays. Even the mass media can initiate family discussions with some of their viewers and listeners, albeit in a vicarious way. Their own family life still has more impact, however, than anything people can see or hear about, and not infrequently the mass media create more misunderstandings and insecurity than their authors and directors could imagine. Their messages are pervaded with pseudoinformation and ideologies that the listeners or viewers cannot always sift out.

One more word about the provider of family therapy. Obviously, he or she should be well qualified. As a rule that means a treatment predicated on classical psychotherapy. The family therapist should have fulfilled all the training requirements of family therapy. He or she should have conducted family therapy under supervision and should regularly attend team conferences with other therapists even after training in order to further improve his understanding of family problems and steadily check on his own modes of understanding family members and of intervention in the process of family therapy. To listen to family members until they feel understood is an integral part of family therapy. Only thereafter, if at all, should exercises of any kind be suggested or advice and instructions given to the family.

EXAMPLE OF A FAMILY THERAPY SESSION

In order to illustrate the complex process of family therapy in action, a portion of a family session is rendered herein verbatim. Nonverbal expressions of the clients have been mentioned when they were unusually obvious or an essential supplement to the spoken word. Some of the impressions, considerations, and thoughts of the family therapist have been presented in the right column of the page and at approximately the place in the discourse where they actually occurred. These impressions and thoughts were, of course, not expressed by the family therapist; at no time did they impede the discourse. They will, perhaps, help the reader understand the therapist's interventions. The reader is recommended to try out other possible interventions in his mind and compare them with those of the family therapist.

First Session

Mrs. M. is looking for help at the family counseling center because she wants to separate from her husband. She mentions that she has a 6-year-old daughter and a 3-year-old son who does not as yet talk. Her husband is manager of a hotel, she is a housewife. They do a lot of entertaining as part of her husband's business. Her husband is willing to come to the family center with her. She would rather leave her children at home. She has a nurse for the children four days of the week.

Mr. and Mrs. M. arrive for the first session in the early afternoon. Mrs. M. is dressed elegantly, if somewhat conspicuously; she wears makeup, is of medium height, and fairly attractive looking, presumably a little over 30 years of age. Mr. M. is also of medium height, very good looking, and conservatively dressed. He appears to be younger than she, but, in fact, he is probably her age or a bit older. They introduce themselves to the therapist and sit down in comfortable armchairs opposite the therapist. Between them there is a low round table with an ashtray. One side wall is covered by a curtain. Behind it, on shelves, there are children's toys. Mrs. M. is looking around the room, Mr. M. at the therapist (Th.).

Th. (after a while): What seems to be the matter?

Mrs. M.: I don't know with whom I talked on the telephone and what the lady told you a few days ago.

Th. (extends his arm and hands a little, looks at Mr. M., then at Mrs. M. again and waits).

Mrs. M. should tell it again so that Mr. M. will hear it too.

Mrs. M.: We may have a retarded child. And we are also having trouble with each other (she motions toward Mr. M.).

Mr. M.: We have two children, Inge, and Peter, and Peter can't talk yet. That is what my wife calls retarded, but Peter actually understands all you want to tell him. He is skillful with his hands, physically strong, and of normal height, our pediatrician says.

Mr. M. seems to like Peter.

Th.: You and your wife are of different opinions on that?

Mrs. M.: Not really. I call him retarded. One could also call him a moron.

Mrs. M. is annoyed at Peter.

Th. (looking at Mr. M.): You agree?

Mr. M.: I don't think he is a moron. He probably has psychological reasons for not talking. I would want to know them. Our pediatrician doesn't think he's retarded. She thinks his intelligence is average. (Turns to Mrs. M.): You're the only one who says that. Why should he be a moron when Inge is highly intelligent?

Mrs. M. (to Mr. M.): That's no guarantee that the second child can't be a moron. You don't think much of genetic makeup, do you? Everything is psychological. This is ridiculous. You have your own reasons, Sir. . . .

Does Mrs. M. hold Mr. M. responsible for Peter's handicap?

Th. (looks at Mr. M., waits for a possible answer and asks him at last): Do you have reasons?

Mr. M.: I have scientific reasons. At least I think that there are scientific reasons, but my wife is probably referring to something else.

Mr. M. tries hard to be objective and reasonable.

Th. (looking at Mrs. M.): True?

Mrs. M.: He can tell you himself if he's so sure of what I have in mind.

Th. (looking at Mr. M., then at Mrs. M., after a while): I for one don't know it.

Tell me about it, both of you!

Mr. M.: I was an illegitimate child. I never knew my father. My wife thinks something was the matter with him and that Peter's defect is from him.

Mrs. M. (pointing at Mr. M.): His mother is no intellectual giant, either, but his father suffered from moral insanity.

Does she think Mr. M. has inferior ancestors?

Th. (looks in an inquiring manner at Mrs. M., then at Mr. M., then again at Mrs. M.)

Mr. M.: My father was said to have been a member of the SS. My mother was an ethnic German born in Hungary. After the war we moved via Austria to Germany.

"Evil soldier" knocks up "good girl"?

Th.: Who is "we"?

Mr. M.: My mother and I. First my mother worked as a cleaning woman, then as a saleswoman, and finally for Lufthansa.

His mother seems to have been a real good girl.

Mrs. M. (with a slight sneer): She looks after the meals.

Mrs. M. does not like her mother-in-law?

Th.: Does she? What do you mean?

Mrs. M. (pointing at Mr. M.): That's *his* field.

Th. (looking at Mr. M., then at Mrs. M.): Which is?

Mr. M.: She is responsible for the passenger catering. She helps to put the menus together and deals with the caterers.

Quite a career, it seems.

Th. (to Mrs. M.): Is that what you meant by "looking after the meals" and "his field," your husband's field?

How does Mrs. M. view her husband's job?

Mrs. M.: More or less. Philip is in the hotel business. He provides for his guests. He likes to sniff around in the kitchen. He's a better cook than I am.

She doesn't think much of his job.

Mr. M.: I wouldn't say that, but I don't mind doing the cooking myself on occasion. Many men don't do that, or they don't want to do it. Hertha doesn't like to cook, but she can cook when she wants to.

He doesn't mind doing something "unmanly"?

Th. (to Mr. M.): And your mother also looks after meals and guests? (Looking at Mrs. M.): She takes care of the passengers?

Mrs. M.: Sort of . . . .

Th. (after a little pause): And what else did you say about her: She's no "intellectual giant"?

Mrs. M. should say more about her rivalry feelings vis-à-vis her mother-in-law.

Mrs. M.: Well . . . at least she has no intellectual interests. All she cares about is her work and her Philip. That was her sole purpose in life. That way she also got him into the hotel business.

She thinks his mother is only interested in her son and not in her.

Mr. M.: My mother got me nowhere. She has helped me financially. She paid for my studies. I haven't lived with her since I was 20. I studied business adminis-

The danger of clinging to Mother too strongly after the loss of Father (and of possible homosexual tendencies) seems to have been overcome.

tration, took a job after I got my diploma, and changed jobs when I got a better offer.

Th.: You work in a hotel?

Mr. M.: I manage hotel G, and I am on the board of directors of the hotel chain.

Mr. M. (too) has had quite a career, it seems. Is Mrs. M. annoyed at that?

Th. (to Mrs. M.): Are you engaged in that too?

Mrs. M. (with a disparaging gesture): Not really. Sometimes I'm the hostess at receptions. Occasionally I help . . .

Yes, she seems irritated.

Th.: But?

Mrs. M.: But what?

Th.: I was under the impression that you have reservations about it.

Mrs. M.: That's his business (pointing at Mr. M.) and he flourishes in it. I look after the household and the children and long for other things than hotel receptions and setting the table.

She despises him and his work.

Th.: What do you long for?

Mrs. M.: I like the theater and concerts. I love to read,

She loves cultivated and pleasurable occupations.

read literature, not business reports and business sections in the papers. I'm interested in the visual arts. I love paintings, exhibitions, and museums.

Th.: You and your husband have interests that you think are not quite compatible?

Mrs. M.: You're putting it mildly. We have no interests in common at all, not only in artistic things.

Th.: You have intellectual and cultural interests and you (looking at Mr. M.) have business interests?

Mr. M.: That's not all. I'm interested in the theater and concerts too. I treasure classical music more than modern music, though, and plays as well. To my mind the so-called modern ones are crazy, but Hertha loves that. The crazier and the more fantastic, the better for her. That's nothing to me. I like to relax and enjoy life. I'm also interested in science, but for recreation after a long day's

Let us state the situation and see.

How far-reaching are their differences of interest?

Jealous?

work I prefer easy enter-
tainment. And I like to be
sociable with people whom
I understand and who are
realistic in their outlook on
life. Hertha is fond of ge-
niuses, of theater folks, and
offbeat painters. I'm not
even sure whether she
hasn't had a love affair with
one of those beatniks.

Th. (looks at Mrs. M., then
at Mr. M.)

Mrs. M. (to Mr. M.): This is
the first time I have heard of
that. Since the subject is up
for discussion, I'd like to
remind you of your dear
little secretary, Mrs. K. I
was suspicious before you
were. I think you are
having an affair with her,
and perhaps with a few
other little girls in the hotel
business, the waitress who
serves the breakfast or one
of those nice little guest-
workers who cleans out the
bathtubs and makes the
beds. Those girls are
suckers for a chance to go to
bed with the manager. I
even have the impression
that you're more infatuated

Is she jealous, too? At any
rate, she is telling him off.
She even suspects him of
homosexuality as an expla-
nation for his lack of love.

with your rowing club than a man should be. (To Th.): Isn't my Philip a handsome man? Women *and* men can't help falling in love with something like that. Let them be happy with him. (Turning to Mr. M.): What you offer, not in terms of money, that's all right, but in terms of interest and understanding—that's not enough for me.

Th. (after a short pause, to Mr. M.): Have you, too, never heard that before?

Mr. M.: No. At the beginning of our married life, or rather after we had our first child, she used to say such things, and (turning to Mrs. M.) when Peter was born I heard it again. You were really cross with me. I'd just taken a new job. That was no easy time for me. But since then (turning to Th.) we've talked less and less to each other except when in company. In fact, we're not talking to each other at all anymore. Sometimes I try to say something but she just shrugs it off. We occa-

He seems to know her complaints. He regrets that they hardly talk to each other and he too complains about her lack of love for him.

sionally discuss domestic matters, the bank account, or when Mrs. Reisinger comes. . . . (Looking at Mrs. M. pensively): Too little interest and understanding? Have *you* got any interest or understanding in *me*?

Mrs. M.: I had . . . Once upon a time. (To Th.): That was when he won me over. I had other friends, one of them for a long time. He wanted to marry me but then this gentleman stepped in (pointing at Mr. M.), courted me, and introduced me to his mother, who advised him against me. I introduced him to my parents, who urged me to choose him, and so the drama took its natural course. (To Mr. M.): At that time you were very attractive. You wanted to be loved and were willing to do something for it.

Mr. M. was not her only candidate for marriage. *His* mother loved him more than her, but *her* parents may have loved him more than her too. Did they want to marry her off? This may be Mrs. M.'s tacit suspicion, if my hunch is borne out.

Mr. M.: I still do a few things for you without much chance of being loved for it, but I still do it. I provide for the house and the children. You've even

Does he mean: "I am doing my duty even without your love"?

had a woman to look after them so that you can breathe. You need to be able to breathe, you said, didn't you?

Mrs. M.: But first you gave me the children.

A bitter rebuke.

Mr. M.: It's what you wanted. I wanted children myself, but not quite so fast. You wanted a child. You wanted a girl at any price, I remember, and I even gave you that.

He reminds her of the truth?

Mrs. M. (to Th.): Does it make any sense for us to quarrel in front of you about what once happened? Now things are different. Inge was a good child, easy to handle, my parents' darling, and (turning to Mr. M.) even your mother liked her, if I remember rightly. Then hubris got you or whatever: Another child, hopefully a boy, so that Inge would not be lonely and your name would be preserved, or rather the name of your mother. Big deal! Even that went according to plan, but it was the end of our love

She does not want to hear the "truth." In order to love children one must have been loved, and be loved, oneself, she may secretly believe. Why does she think she has not been loved enough? Is she referring to her parents? Should they get a demonstration of how unhappy they have made her when they "gave" her to Mr. M.?

relationship, if our relationship at that time was still love . . . . Thinking back, your fuss about a son and heir may have had something to do with it. Now you have your heir. See to it that you can get him to speak. Keep him. I'll move to my parents with Inge.

Mr. M. (looks at Mrs. M. in mild disbelief, shakes his head and smiles stiffly).

Th. (after a pause, looking at Mrs. M.): This is obviously how you feel. And you, Mr. M., have never heard her say it so bluntly?

I hear Mrs. M.'s strong statement. Do you, Mr. M.?

Mr. M.: She has hinted at it, but we don't talk about such things . . . . I keep thinking, what would it be like if the children had heard her say all that. That would not be good. That would make them feel quite upset and insecure.

Is he that worried about the children? Or does he plead for consideration for the children in order to keep his wife?

Th. (to Mrs. M.): Do you think so, too?

Mrs. M.: That's a possibility . . . Inge once had a nightmare. I forgot what it was,

but when I took her to kindergarten next morning I
had to promise her that I
would not run away.
Maybe she senses some-
thing, even though I don't
talk about it. What Peter
thinks or senses escapes
me, though.

If *he* is not quite as involved
with the children as *he* pre-
tends, *she* seems to be even
less involved. She cannot
remember Inge's night-
mare? And Peter keeps irri-
tating her.

Th. (to Mr. M.): Have you
got an idea?

How well does *he* under-
stand the children, or Peter?

Mr. M.: From what little I
know about psychology I
could imagine that he no-
tices something of our personal difficulties; or perhaps of his mother's
feelings toward him. *She*
resents him, I think, and
that's what he notices. *I*
don't resent him, at least I
believe not, but I'm not
home much. Mrs. Reisinger
does not resent him either,
but she may be a bit at a loss
over his not talking. I have
the impression that some-
times she wants to get him
to talk and is disappointed
when he can't or refuses to.

"Mrs. Reisinger under-
stands the children. That is
good. Perhaps she can save
our family life," Mr. M.
may be implying.

Th. (to Mrs. M.): *Do* you feel that you resent Peter emotionally?

A hard accusation that she has permission to deny.

Mrs. M.: How can a mother resent her own children? I don't resent Peter. Yet he made my life much harder than Inge did. I'm annoyed that he can't talk. That's why I sometimes even avoid him and leave him to Mrs. Reisinger.

Subjectively she has not had an easy time.

Th.: If I understand it correctly, Peter expresses himself vocally, but he doesn't talk. He doesn't use words?

How grave is Peter's defect? He is not deaf, is he?

Mrs. M.: He can sing. Hum, I should say, because he doesn't open his mouth as he sings.

She is annoyed even at that.

Mr. M.: He remembers tunes.

He praises Peter.

Mrs. M.: Inge remembered tunes, too, at that age, but she could sing them. On her third birthday she knew twenty children's songs including the texts. For the fun of it we checked and counted them. This was a little before my second baby.

She praises Inge.

Th. (To Mrs. M.): Did you know those children's songs yourself?

Mrs. M.: All those songs were songs I knew as a child. My mother sang them for Inge. I'm no great singer.

Th.: And who sang for Peter?

Mrs. M.: My mother.

Mr. M.: And Inge. I think Peter has learned more from Inge than he did from your mother.

Mrs. M.: Not that I know. The children hardly play with each other. Inge is in kindergarten. Peter is dumbly playing along by himself.

Mr. M.: Mrs. Reisinger tells me that the children often play together. I often see them doing things together.

Mrs. M.: I had to comfort Inge once when Peter had messed up her dolls. He

Who taught Inge those songs? Perhaps we can hear a little about Mrs. M.'s own childhood.

"My mother helped me. Does she love Inge more than she does me?" Mrs. M. might be wondering. Has her mother helped with Peter, too?

Even Inge helped Mrs. M.?

Does Mrs. M. not even want her children to play with each other?

Trespassing among siblings. That's not uncommon.

had broken the head off one of them. Inge was afraid of Peter. She wanted a key for her room so that she could lock him out.

Mr. M.: She never used the key.

Who is speaking the truth?

Mrs. M.: How do you know?

Mr. M.: She gave it to Mrs. Reisinger for her to keep in my desk. I found it there the other day and asked Mrs. Reisinger about it.

Mr. M. appears to have the true story.

Mrs. M.: Then why did she want the key to begin with? Mrs. Reisinger should tell me too . . . . I think I remember. Well, thinking back . . . to be truthful, I have never found Inge's room locked.

Mrs. M. is surprised. She indicates, chagrined, that she is willing to take a lesson. She admits something that proves Mr. M. right.

Th. (after a short pause): Apparently Inge was not so afraid of Peter?

Does Mrs. M. recognize that she may have been misjudging Inge? That she herself feels the way she thinks Inge feels?

Mrs. M.: I can't quite imagine that. Don't all children dread their little brothers and sisters at times?

She tries to justify herself.

Th.: Do you have experiences of your own in that regard?

Mrs. M.: When I was pregnant I asked myself how Inge would take to a little brother or sister. We didn't tell her until the very last minute, when I was almost ready to go to the clinic. Inge was completely naive. She had no idea what was going on.

Was Mrs. M. more afraid of the second child than Inge?

Th.: What I meant was experiences in your own childhood?

She does not want to speak of her own feelings?

Mrs. M.: Experiences of what kind?

Th.: With younger brothers and sisters?

Mrs. M.: I have no brothers and sisters. I am the only one . . . that is . . . wait a minute . . . . If I'm not mistaken, my mother had a miscarriage or rather a premature birth. The child was born alive, but died within an hour.

A little surprise that she happens to provide herself with. She almost had a sibling, but this had been forgotten.

Th.: How old were you then?

Mrs. M.: I hadn't been born yet. That was before my time.

Her potential sibling would have been older than she. As a consequence of that miscarriage her parents may have pampered her.

Th.: Was the child a boy or a girl?

Mrs. M.: Can one tell? With a premature baby ... I don't know. . . . I think it was a boy, but this was never talked about. How come I know about it at all?

She is not sure what sex the sibling would have been. Did she herself, not Inge, not want to have a sibling (a brother)?

Mr. M.: I've never heard of it before.

This is news for Mr. M., too.

Th. (after a long pause): Could it be that you're drawing on some frightening experiences of your own in childhood, or perhaps just frightening possibilities—not actual experiences, but possible dangers—when you try to think of Inge's situation after her little brother had arrived?

Let me try an interpretation, with caution. She can reject it, if it is too much for her.

Mrs. M. (after a short pause, pensively): You think I'm imagining things? I had a wonderful childhood. My parents doted on

She senses something, feels something but, for now, wards it off. She digresses to Peter, Mr. M. and their current problems.

me, especially my father. He was crazy about me, I'm told. . . . Something frightening? Are you implying that my mother's miscarriage may have frightened me? I knew nothing about it. I think I learned about it only as a teenager or later. What could that have to do with Peter's handicap? And our troubles (pointing to Mr. M.)? Our relationship is no good anymore. What are we going to do? Should we separate or stay together without love, just for the sake of the children?

Mr. M.: There could well be a connection. Your relationship with Peter is strained. He has done you no harm, but you don't like him. You almost damn him. You have no rational attitude toward him.

Does he want to support me? He senses more than she does. It's easier for him. It's not his problem, but hers (although he has problems of his own). He even scolds her.

Mrs. M.: (annoyedly): To make it rational, I would have to study business administration, I guess. Would that suit you?

She defends herself against his reproaches.

Th. (pausing for a moment): Here we can discuss the problems and possibilities that you (looking at Mrs. M.) have mentioned: Separation or staying together; what to do with the children if you separate; your relationships with the children, and of the children among themselves. (Looking at both of them): We might look at your relationships with each of your parents and try to clarify them.

A little summary and instruction about what they can expect in family therapy that may be helpful to them.

Mr. M.: You mean our relationship to her parents (pointing at Mrs. M.) and to my mother?

He objects to the fact that his (unknown) father might be drawn into it, too.

Th.: Yes, but (looking at Mr. M.) even your father has a role irrespective of whether you knew him or not. You've mentioned him already yourself.

Mrs. M.: Well . . . is that getting us anywhere?

She expresses skepticism.

Th.: According to my experiences, yes, but you can see for yourself. If it does not help you (looking at both of them), you're free of

She has permission to express skepticism. Some further instruction about the therapy situation seems indicated.

course to try something else. I might be able to help you even at that. But to see for yourself you wouldhave to try it for a certain time.

Mr. M.: What time?

Does he think of the costs?

Th.: For a few sessions at first. Then you can make up your mind yourselves whether you want to continue. I, in turn, might be able to advise you whether from my point of view you should continue.

Don't be afraid, Mr. and Mrs. M.! If it gets to be too much for you or if it does not help you, *I* am at fault, not *you*.

During the rest of this session Mrs. M.'s family, the beginnings of Mr. and Mrs. M.'s relationship with each other and a few details of Inge's early childhood were discussed.

Diagnostic Evaluation

Both Mr. and Mrs. M. grew up as single children. This leads one to expect that handling children and rearing them will not be easy for either of them, unless conditions in their families of origin were exceptionally favorable, and that is quite unlikely to have been the case with Mr. M. He had no father, and we have not heard about a substitute father or grandparent who might have compensated for him. His mother was engaged in an uphill struggle for a livelihood and eventually succeeded remarkably. A strong bond that undoubtedly exists between her and her son keeps the son psychologically more dependent on his mother, at least far more than are sons in intact families. His interest in women may be stunted, and homosexual tendencies could arise.

The hard struggle for life that Mr. M. and his mother had to endure may have reduced those dangers. Mr. M. was able to separate from his mother in due time, to hold his own at his studies and at work—he is in a managerial position in a reputable firm—and he has obviously been seriously interested in women. In courting Mrs. M., he had to contend with at least one strong competitor. This is not to say, however, that all the dangers mentioned have indeed disappeared from Mr. M.'s life.

In all likelihood, Mrs. M. had a much better childhood and youth, although her family may have suffered from war-related and postwar hardships, too. The miscarriage suffered by Mrs. M.'s mother before she was born may have made her parents overprotective of her. Her happiness and well-being were conceivably of utmost importance to the parents. If the miscarried child was indeed a boy, as Mrs. M. seems to remember, the parents may also have regretted that they had not had another son.

If such a regret had ever been voiced or had otherwise been noticed by her, Mrs. M. would probably have felt quite hurt. In fact, unconsciously she may have tried to protect herself against another hurt like that. It could be that the family contemplated another child, but she resented the idea. Perhaps her memory fooled her and the miscarriage was after she had been born. At any rate, she seems to have brought an aversion against a second child into her marriage. Maybe she did not want children at all, in spite of her expressed wish to the contrary. Her desire for a daughter as soon as she was married could have been an indication of her feeling of being loved too little, not only by her husband, but even by her parents. This unfulfilled need could be corrected by having a girl and loving her the way she, Mrs. M., would have wanted to be loved.

In other words, in spite of the favorable circumstances in which Mrs. M. grew up, Mrs. M. may have brought to her marriage no great disposition for handling and rearing children. This aversion could perhaps have been camouflaged in the case of her first child, Inge, particularly since Inge is said to have been an exceptionally bright child. When the second child arrived, and a boy of barely average capacity to boot, her distress became apparent. She herself wanted to be the child or, being a mother, to get much more recognition, admiration, and praise than she actually earned on behalf of the children. She felt that if she had been "handed over to a man" who *did* give her a child, he would have to apologize for all those slights and offenses by an excess of love. If he failed to provide that love, he ought to bear and feel the consequences—and Peter too.

This conflict between the parents and their children as well as the aggravation of this conflict caused by the arrival of Peter might have retarded Peter's speech development. Even if there were an organic defect in Peter, the tension between the parents and the rejection by his mother may have had reinforcing effects. If nothing of substance was talked about in the family, Inge and Peter must have noticed the chilled, uncommunicative atmosphere prevailing between the parents and worried about whether the family would last.

In family therapy the relationships of Mr. and Mrs. M. to their respective parents and their family histories can be explored and investigated for their contributions—through transference—to their own partner conflict. It is conceivable that both of them are psychologically more dependent on their parents or mother than they are aware of and that they would have loved to get more attention and help from them than was the case. For that, however, Mrs. M. would have had to recognize and curb her jealousy of her mother-in-law.

The children, Inge and Peter, seem to have a fairly undisturbed relationship with each other. Of all possible people Inge may be the first to get Peter to talk. Perhaps

Peter has already spoken to Inge. The parents should be encouraged not to interfere to any great extent in the children's relationship with each other. What they might do, if they can, is observe the children quietly and perhaps even learn from them a few things that they did not learn in their own childhood—a few things that might be useful in their marriage and that would serve everyone's needs. Perhaps Mrs. M. would even give up her idea of moving to her parents.

The children should not be separated, even if the parents insist on separation. If the parents realize, though, that their children would be traumatized by their parents' separation, Mrs. M., in particular might become more serious and practical in contemplating their options. In this process, other people whom Mr. and Mrs. M. had considered as candidates for love and marriage before they married each other could come up for discussion and may help to illuminate their actual choice of partner. They may learn more clearly why they chose each other, what they could not seem to get from other potential partners, or what they might have gotten from the relationship if only that partner had not turned elsewhere. Discussing these feelings might make them try to work out their problems.

All recommendations for treatment are valid only on condition that we have adequately understood and interpreted the clients, their communications, feelings, and circumstances of life that they reported and displayed. If contradictory information should emerge in future sessions, the tentative portrait sketched and course of therapy would have to be adjusted.

As part of a follow-up years later, the reader may be interested to learn that Mr. and Mrs. M. did come for some thirty-five weekly sessions, one and one-half hours each, the last five of them after a year's intermission. They brought Peter along twice. Although Inge could not come the first time because of a prior invitation to a children's party, she was reported to have commented to her parents before the second session when nothing prevented her from coming, "You go and I'll stay home. You can tell me about it later." This remark sounded to the parents and therapist as if she was implying that there was nothing wrong with her or Peter, but her parents were having a problem.

By that time Peter had begun to talk to Inge, to his grandmother and to Mrs. Reisinger, and it soon became evident that he could speak almost as well as other children his age, but he continued to say very little. In the two sessions Peter attended he played by himself in a corner of the room but occasionally stopped as if to listen to the conversation. At one point Mr. M. asked him whether he wanted to move closer to them, whereupon Peter said "No." That word was all he ever said in the sessions, but at home he talked more and more often.

The parents arranged for Mr. M. to have a small apartment of his own and to come for regular weekend visits. Mother and children stayed in the house. There had indeed been some extramarital activities on Mr. M.'s part in which, however, he began to lose interest. He also brought several of his more fantastic career ideas, such as becoming a business tycoon in underdeveloped countries, back to earth. He grew more attentive of his wife, and she, in turn, became less bitchy and more interested in others, including her children and husband. What precipitated the parents more sober and mature behavior was a marriage offer to Mr. M.'s mother from an elderly well-to-do gentleman. At first this proposal of marriage upset Mr. M. unduly, and after some turbulence and irrational outbursts on Mr. M.'s part, it eventually brought Mr. and Mrs. M. closer together.

An inquiry four years after termination of therapy revealed that Inge was doing excellent work in school, whereas Peter was only an average student. Peter was still not very talkative, and his behavior was inconspicuous except for a tendency to show off in physical activities and sports. Mr. M. had moved back into the house. Both Mr. and Mrs. M. claimed that they were getting along with each other much better than before.

Can One Generalize?

One could argue that the M. family life is rather civilized, that the parents are well-to-do, have no financial worries to speak of, and are both well educated and rather intelligent. What can be done, though, with families living in poverty and distress, who have no education, who feed and embrace each other, are envious, indulgent, who may steal from each other, beat each other, or run away and come back, but do not talk with one another? What does one do with families who are scattered, with incomplete families, with persons who have lost all contact with family members, or, even worse, who never had a family life? Would it not be better to subsidize them with some regular allowance, to give them better living quarters, or coach their children for school? Would not some of those families have to be shown what family life should be like and practice it under guidance?

Those are legitimate questions. There are distresses other than psychic ones, even if the majority of families in Western Europe or in North America are in no material need. The misery of families who have been decimated and/or split up needs help other than family therapy. On the other hand, the psychic distress that accompanies physical need and misery is by no means coincidental. Family therapists can be useful even to broken and impoverished families. To begin with, they can help them search for medical, financial, and material aid and utilize the assistance already offered. Ultimately, they can help them to help themselves. They may even give them instructions for a better family life and help them practice those instructions. That means that they are acting not only as family therapists but also as advisors and teachers of positive cooperative family living. They can even get those persons who have never had a family life to develop one of their own. This is done partly by concrete recommendations for the patients' daily life, sometimes even by orders and active changes in the life contexts of the client family.

In all such instances, however, the classical family therapist has explored the situation first in accordance with classical therapy rules. During that exploration phase family members have been expressing themselves the way they wanted and dared to and have been listening to each other long enough to learn something new about other family members. They discover something about each other's experiences, thoughts, wishes, or interests that they had not known before or had not perceived that way. This is possible even with families who cannot express themselves very well in speech and who do not understand verbal communications of their family members. Even such families hear, articulate, and understand more through language than the passing observer appears to recognize—ordinarily even more than they can communicate to each other in other cruder and physical ways.

That is to say, even those supposedly inarticulate families are not immune to family therapists' comments and interpretations—although they should be offered on the particular family's level of understanding and in their language or idiom. Such families can often provide each other with insightful interpretations, if need be, without any institutional family therapy. Furthermore, without some insight into the feelings, motives, and conflicts of family members (even if it is only one such insight), the family cannot effect change. Without such change or at least the beginning of change in family relationships and outlook of family members, any material help offered often does not serve the intended purpose. It merely is wasted or cynically abused.

ANOTHER EXAMPLE OF FAMILY THERAPY

The Williams family wanted to begin family therapy. Before making their first appointment, the secretary of the family therapy center had secured some basic information about the family over the telephone using a small family questionnaire:

- Mr. W. was the younger brother of a sister who had married but remained childless. Mr. W.'s father was the oldest of three boys, and Mr. W.'s mother the youngest sister of two older brothers.

- Mrs. W. was an only child, her mother a younger sister of a sister, her father the younger brother of two sisters.

- Mr. W. was 52 years old, Mrs. W. 40. They had two daughters, Jean who was 19 years old, and Liz 16.

In symbolic form their family constellation could be written as such:

	Jean	Liz	
Mr. W.'s parents	Mr. W.	Mrs. W.	Mrs. W.'s parents

$$b(bb) \: / \: (bb)s \: / \: / \: (s)b_{52} \: / \: s_{19} \: s_{16} \: / \: s_{40} \: / \: / \: (ss)b \: / \: (s)s$$

Attempt at a Blind Diagnosis

These structural features suggested to the therapist the following theoretical portrait of the Williams family. Some readers may want to just skim through this section or skip it altogether for the time being. What is important to illustrate, though, is what experienced family therapists, especially those with a psychoanalytic understanding and a sensitivity to the social contexts and family backgrounds in which all human life originates, tend to think about beforehand or as the therapeutic process begins to evolve (see also Toman 1961, 1965).

As a younger brother of a sister Mr. W. may have wanted all the nurturing he could get for himself in order to do whatever he pleased and devote himself to his work and to his hobbies. His children were his wife's job and legacy; he could not be bothered too much. Through identification with his father (probably a leader of men or at least of his brothers) and through interaction with his mother (who may have wanted men including her husband and her son to be like her brothers) Mr. W. is also likely to have adopted attitudes of leadership and care with respect to dependents, including his wife, that conflicted with his early experiences as a younger brother of a sister. This may have resulted in his alternating between overdoing and underdoing his responsibilities as a caring father rather than fulfilling them appropriately as each situation demanded. His leadership may have appeared arbitrary at times, and his caring not entirely natural or steady.

For her part, Mrs. W., as an only child, would rather be on the receiving end of parental attention and responsibility than doling it out, one might expect. Through identification with her mother (a younger sister of a sister), she could not have learned very much about caring and nursing. Mrs. W.'s mother would have wanted to lean on someone, perhaps assert herself on occasion and argue her point of view on certain issues. She would rather have wanted to be understood by another person than try to understand him or her. What's more, Mrs. W.'s father had a similar predicament in his early life. He was used to being looked after by his older sisters and he unconsciously longed for an older sister for a wife, but apparently he got a younger sister instead.

Both of Mrs. W.'s parents, then, were in want of leadership. They hoped for someone to nurture and guide them, someone who would tell them what to do, a person whom they could fall back on and, unfortunately, they could not help each other in that respect. If they did not find such a person among their friends or relatives, they might even look to their own child for all that. In other words, without being shown by her parents, Mrs. W. may have been unconsciously urged by her parents to become their guardian and confidante. Whether a young person can really fulfill such expectations and whether she can learn by indirection what it is that her parents want her to be remains a question. Yet on the surface Mrs. W. may have succeeded. She may have become a Pygmalion-type older sister for her father and mother, and that part of Mrs. W. might have been, among other things, what beguiled Mr. W. when he courted her.

Such anticipations, however, might have been counteracted by Mr. and Mrs. W.'s age difference of twelve years. She was quite young when they married, perhaps 19 or 20. No one including himself would expect him to take anything other than a protective and paternal role vis-à-vis his wife.

The therapist noted also in his mind that Mr. W. is used to living with a peer of the other sex (he had an older sister), and so was his mother (who had older brothers). Mrs. W., on the other hand, as an only child, was not accustomed to life with a peer of the other sex (or with any peer, for that matter), nor was her mother (who had just an older sister). At least her father had the experience of growing up with older sisters.

The spouse who is more experienced in living with the other sex is likely to teach the less experienced. Hence Mr.

W. would tend to teach Mrs. W. In addition, their age difference may have given their relationship a touch of Father and Daughter. Yet, if Mr. W. does indeed feel called upon to assume a fatherly role toward his wife (which, as an only child, she might have invited), the example he could readily follow would be that of his own father. In reality, that man, however, was the oldest brother of brothers. Mr. W., therefore, when acting fatherly, may treat his wife somewhat like a boy. He may be harder on her than she would like or comfortably endure. He may also tend to be hard on his daughters and could be expected to feel that at least one of the children should have been a boy.

The children, Jean and Liz, are likely to have had some difficulties on account of those hidden conflicts within each of their parents and were probably witness to some overt conflict between the parents, too. The older girl, Jean, may have been called upon unconsciously by her father and mother to act like an older sister not only for Liz but for them as well. There could have been traces even of parental jealousy of Jean's attention to their respective interests and wishes.

Liz, in contrast, could identify with her mother or, more precisely speaking, with "mother's mother within mother," and with father as a youngest sibling. Somehow, though, Liz may have sensed that her parents do not permit themselves to be what they immaturely want to be. She sensed perhaps that they are conflicted about some of their own dearest wishes. Hence Liz may have concluded that she should do likewise, even if she found full parental support at first for living it up or at least for fulfilling her own dearest wishes. Liz may resolve that she should not do that.

Both daughters were adolescents at the time the family was seeking therapeutic help. Hopefully, Jean has had sufficient opportunities to have contact with boys and test her interests. By now she can possibly look back on some

experiences with one or several boys and also on her parents'
reactions to those experiences. They might be reluctant to let
her branch out into a social environment of which they are
no part because they are afraid of losing her.

Conceivably, the younger daughter Liz is in the beginning stages of exploring her love interests more realistically.
Watching her parents and Jean's conflicts over Jean's love
interests and growing absences from home, both physically
and psychologically, Liz could have become aware that she
now will either have to shed her parents and live her own life
regardless of their disapproval or knuckle under their neurotic needs by disallowing her own budding love wishes
more vehemently than she had thus far.

It looks as if either daughter could be the identified
patient in the family. However, Liz, may, at first, have been
encouraged by her parents to be herself, that is, to be a
younger sister, but with subsequent unease over the ambiv-
alences within her parents about urging her to be carefree,
(to which she was becoming acutely aware as she grew
older) she may even be more vulnerable to parental pressures than Jean.

If Mr. W. assumed a strong role as a father, he may be
communicating unwittingly that he would prefer his daughters, or at least one of them, to be like boys. Girls are fine, if
they take care of men. If they don't or can't, they have to be
managed, subjected to a man's control, or even transformed
into some kind of male personalities or genderless being.
That could be one of the conflicts that the identified patient
in the family W., presumably Liz rather than Jean, finds
herself stuck with: she should behave like a boy and must
not act like a woman, no matter how interesting and attractive boys may have appeared to her in her childhood and
early teens. She must berate herself whenever she feels
tempted. Otherwise, she can never hope to win her father's
approval. Approval is all one can hope for when love has

become so loaded with parental pressures. She believes Father cannot love her as a girl.

Those readers who have followed the therapist's conjectures about the structural properties of the Williams family with impatience and incredulity or even skipped some or most of it should not reread the preceding until it becomes more plausible but, rather, just go on. Further details of the family history and family life as well as of the psychotherapeutic process will make the Williams family more vivid, colorful, and understandable and their problems more transparent. If the reader wishes, he or she can come back to the therapist's a priori conjectures thereafter.

Those readers who have tried to follow the therapist's reasoning closely and were able to make sense of it, however, should not stick to it compulsively or try to rehearse it before continuing to read. Whatever they have retained of it spontaneously will be good enough, even if it feels inconsequential. I recommend that those readers just let the coming story unfold before them. Whether the therapist's reasoning before the facts, or at least before most of the facts, has been valid can be subsequently checked by all readers.

The Family History and the Course of Therapy

The Williams family came to weekly sessions with an occasional two-week interval. Often all four of them attended. However, all of them except Mrs. W. had, after a while, missed sessions, and Mr. W. the most. At first he had excused himself repeatedly on grounds of business commitments but was urged politely by Mrs. W., and more bluntly by Jean, to make a greater effort to come. Eventually even Liz chimed in with some trepidation, but by that time Mr. W. was attending regularly.

In the early sessions the family dwelt on their daily

chores and conflicts, both present and past. Father was always very busy and not really available even when he was at home. Mother had to keep an impeccable home, not so much of her own accord as upon the insistence of Father. In quarrels that the daughters overheard at home Father always came out on top with Mother intimidated and occasionally crying. She would try to hide it, though.

Father was interested in the daughters' schoolwork but in little else. They had tried in their childhood to engage him in play, especially when it was doll play, but he ran out of patience too quickly and sometimes expressed his irritation. Wasn't there something more interesting they would want to play, like chess, perhaps, or bridge, he would argue jokingly. They did not like either, partly because they were too young when he had first tried to teach them. Mother's refusal to play chess and her reluctance to play bridge—she did so only for the guests' sake—may have had something to do with it. Among the few things with which the daughters could capture their father's interest was playing tag and wrestling. The girls loved it, but even with such physical play he would stop after a while. At wrestling he would stop playtime by holding both of them in locks at the same time, which, according to the rules of the game, signified the end. They had been defeated. In playing tag he would not catch them at first, but as soon as his patience ran out he would tag them, quickly and almost frighteningly so, usually long before Jean and Liz had had their fill.

In a way, though, they had enjoyed being frightened by Father at play. Sometimes they would egg him on to play monster. They sometimes got really scared, including Mother, and the girls would scream. It would end by Father snapping out of the monster act and hugging them. The girls loved that part of the game. Mother commented in one of the sessions that those were the only sincere hugs Father had given them. He was kind and tender when the girls were anxious or depressed. When they were small and in tears, he was always able to cheer them up. Later on, however, he would call them crybabies, even though there was not much crying at all in the family. He would scold them rather than comfort them on those rare occasions when they did show unhappiness. More often they did not display disappointment or sadness, Mother claimed, but on the whole they were happy children. Their troubles began only later or perhaps they just became noticeable, she volunteered.

At bedtime the daughters had wanted the father to tell them stories, which he could do well, but which he often cut short or began to narrate so annoyingly that after a while they just let him go. Much more often it was Mother who told them stories before they went to sleep or at other times, and her stories were much better than his, Father would declare laughingly. "They are the artists," he said with a gesture at his wife and daughters, whereas he was the scientist. They were the gardeners, with the possible exception of Liz, and he was the engineer. They were the dancers; he was the athlete. Liz was in between, he thought and asked Liz whether she liked to spend time in his basement workshop and to help him, but she denied vehemently that she had wanted to help him. He couldn't be helped because she wasn't good enough for him. She was no good at anything she had ever tried.

In fact, this was far from true. Both daughters had been excellent in school, good at sports, writing little stories, and drawing pictures. The mother had often praised Liz's cartoons and even Father could not help being impressed by them when he took the time to look. Yet, rather than expressing at least some praise he would tell them or show them what they could do to improve their product. They hated his put-downs.

Mother was much more accessible to the children, more patient and quite cooperative, but sometimes there was a sadness about her that upset them. Occasionally, the daughters had wondered whether the cause of it was Father, but Mother would not tell them. She would rather blame herself. She would praise Father as a good provider and disparage herself for being too easily discouraged or hurt. Father does not mean to, she would insist, but in order to make a living for all of them he had to work very hard. His mind was of necessity preoccupied with work. When they entertained guests, Mother had often felt ill at ease. The children had begun to notice her uneasiness as they grew up and gradually took some part in their parents' adult activities. Father, on the other hand, was flamboyant and carefree at those parties, charming the ladies, and earning undivided or envious respect from the men. In that process he often forgot about Mother. To him she was not the hostess, but the maid, and his daughters should help her so that the party would be a success.

Mother had a degree in art history, which,in the eyes of Father, was good for nothing. Before marrying Father she had worked for two years as a secretary for a government agency, something he esteemed much more highly than her interest in art and music. The natural thing for a wife to do, he felt, was to assist men, in particular her husband, at work and in their social life. That was, in fact, what Mother's mother had taught Mother. She had also told her that it was more important for a woman to be loved than to love. There were two other men who had been seriously interested in her besides Father. They were closer to her in age than he,but in her mother's opinion and even in her own they did not amount to much as potential providers. They were still wondering about their own careers, whereas Father, at that time, had been well established in his work as an engineer and was making good money. He seemed to know what he wanted, both in his profession and in their relationship. He promised Mother's mother that he would take good care of

Anna (Mother) and their future children. He expressed to her his desire to have children.

Mother's father also approved of Shep (Father), although when Shep first indicated that he and Anna wanted to marry and were hoping for her parents' approval, Mother's father nearly collapsed. He had been so used to two women looking after him and indulging his every request, Mother explained. In her early years, however, Mother's father had been very disappointed at having a girl, so much so, that he wanted no more children. One could not be sure that they would not be girls, he was known to have complained. Yet when Anna grew up and began to express her eagerness to learn and her curiosity about many things (including biology, art, and history), he became increasingly impressed with her intelligence and gladly let her teach him about a few subjects. He would also proudly show her off among their friends and enjoy her scholarly conversations with some of them.

Father related that he had had a "sissy-period" in childhood. That was when his own mother and even more so his (older) sister had tried to dress him up and make him behave nicely like a girl. In his early teens, perhaps under the influence of his father and uncle (his father's middle brother), and one of his classmates he "broke out of that stuff for good," took to competitive sports (track and mountain climbing), and discovered to his delight that he had a natural ability in the sciences. At one point in his adolescence he contemplated becoming a Buddhist monk. In the therapy it turned out that this was at about the time when his sister got engaged. He claimed it had nothing to do with it, but Mother as well as Jean seemed convinced that it did.

Father's father had been a locksmith who eventually opened up a hardware store with his youngest brother. Father's father and mother had retired some ten years ago and died the year before last in quick succession. Because of distance there was and is not much personal contact with the members of Father's family, but Father has been in touch by phone and occasional letters with both of his paternal uncles. He did not convey much of the conversation to Mother or the children because they were not interested in his family, he alleged, whereas Mother and daughters claimed they were. Liz accused Father of thinking that they, the girls, were not good enough to be informed, or rather too stupid, she once shouted in a session.

Early in the family therapy sessions it became apparent that Liz had been the family's designated patient, although in the very beginning it looked as if the family was upset about Jean and her acting up with boys. She had stayed away overnight, supposedly with girlfriends, and used encounters with her boyfriends to compromise and slander the family, especially Father. Father, in turn, would claim at dinners that Jean was making a fool of herself and was not aware that boys abused and made fun of her. All she got was a reputation as an easy lay, Father was supposed to have said, but he did not remember ever saying that.

Liz had landed her first boyfriend at about that time. He was a handsome boy, but both Father and Mother were unimpressed by his intelligence and his educational interests. It appeared as if the annoyance and deprecation expressed by the parents toward Jean and her behavior with boys had a deep impact on Liz. This was not what Father wanted of his daughters, Liz concluded, and as the (only) man in the family he would know best.

From then on until a year ago, Liz had resolved to stay away from boys altogether. Even more, she stopped indulging herself in anything, even eating. She had been the more active and vivacious of the two girls anyway. She had loved to eat great quantities of food, but she had seemed to work it all off in her numerous vigorous activities. Ever since she and her sister had been told in no uncertain terms how to view Jean's behavior and Liz's first boyfriend, Liz had become afraid of growing fat.

Liz also began to hate herself for menstruating. This was an utter nuisance, she had tacitly concluded and eventually expressed in family therapy. She and her sister had suspected their father of being disappointed at having merely girls. He had wanted a boy, which seemed true enough on the surface. He had joked about such matters and sighed about their lack of interest in physics and mechanical skills, even though they had had no difficulties in science. What better way of pleasing Father than to become a kind of boy oneself. Girls were soft and flabby. Boys were tough. Girls grew fat, whereas boys stayed slim. Girls grew breasts, which were good for nothing. Such were the thoughts of Liz.

About a year before treatment began, Liz had cut down severely on eating, fussed over calories, and eventually refused to eat meat, but gobbled up large quantities of salads, some vegetables, and unripe fruit. One slice of Norwegian flatbread was all the carbohydrates she took in, plus spoonfuls of cottage cheese and skimmed milk for protein. She had turned quite reclusive and quarrelsome when disturbed, but she made a great effort to keep up her grades. She succeeded, yet it was apparent that she was heavily absorbed in her own imagination, fears, and struggles. She broke off almost all contacts with friends.

When her state of health had become critical about four months before family treatment began, both Mother and Father had pleaded with her to see friends more often and to take better care of her health. Liz had screamed back at them that she just did not want to eat the way they did. "If you keep it up that way, you may die," Mother worried. "So what?" Liz replied. "I don't mind dying. You want me to die anyway." Her mother answered, gently, "Where did you get that idea? We want you to live. We are very concerned. You are endangering your life." "Father doesn't," Liz retorted.

At that point her father was so perplexed that he could say nothing, but tears came to his eyes. Mother saw them, whereas Liz was too agitated to focus on anything. Mother was moved by what she saw but was unable to speak either. As the silence continued, Liz was apparently becoming aware that something was going on between the parents. Father eventually said, with a tremor in his voice, "Liz, we want you to live. We want you to be happy. I am at a loss. I don't know anymore how we can help you."

For a moment Liz looked at her Father, but, as she later recalled, she did not see him, nor did she get the meaning of his words. However, she noticed from the tone of his voice that he, "the great, inexorable man," had been shaken. She remembered that it was like a glimpse of light in utter darkness. At the moment, however, she could do nothing but run to her room and lock the door. An hour later the parents heard her cry vehemently, but she would not answer their call nor open the door. From then on, with some conversations between her and Jean, Liz began to eat a little more at first, eventually even in voracious spells. She devoured a bowl of green beans — something she had avoided before "because of their calories" — in one big rush. Another time she gulped a pound of heavy cheese. When she developed stomach cramps after one such feat, Father tried to help her by massaging her belly and relaxing her neck, arms, and legs with quick shakes and gentle strokes as he had experienced them in his own athletic career. He fortunately succeeded in helping her.

During those times Liz also started talking to her mother again and told her some of the horrible dreams that had begun to harass her in which animals and wild people attacked her and others — dreams in which friends occasionally changed into monsters or were disfigured, bled profusely, or died horrible deaths. Telling her mother about them and receiving comments and occasional common sense interpretations, but above all getting comfort and consolation over the rage and guilt that Liz was experiencing, did progressively more to put her at ease, at least temporarily. More and more often Liz cried bitterly in front of her mother and screamed mostly at herself and at other people that had occupied her thoughts and memories. Eventually she clung to her mother in a tight embrace and let Mother hold her and caress her for increasingly longer stretches of time. It looked for a while as if Liz were insatiable for motherly affection and indulgence in her unhappiness and passivity.

As she began to inquire about her Father's courtship of Mother and some incidents of their early relationship, it became evident that Liz had believed all along that Mother was oppressed and maltreated by Father from the beginning of their relationship. Mother objected to that notion, claiming that she and Father had had happy early years together and that it became difficult only as Father's professional life grew more pressing, urgent, and competitive. Liz tried to prove to her mother how inconsiderate Father had been to Mother and provided episodes that demonstrated his recklessness and egotism. Mother did not always agree and could not even remember some episodes, but as they talked about them, Liz began to realize that possibly Father was not all bad.

Much of this had come out in the early sessions of family therapy. Inadvertently or, in other words, by no explicit intent of the therapist the family members reviewed their family history. It seemed that an important therapeutic change had occurred in the Williams family months before they decided to seek psychotherapeutic help for Liz. Half aware Liz may have been terrorizing and trying to punish Father for the scant interest and lack of respect that he showed to girls in general and to Mother and herself in particular. The ultimate motive of her noncaring Father was to be rid of them, she believed. She wanted to take revenge on her Father although unconsciously she was trying to accomplish something else. She was trying to please him by becoming a fleshless, ethereal, beautiful, intelligent, and hard-working nonsexual being. If her efforts failed, she would die in the process and please Father that way. Maybe, he would be sorry for the rest of his life, she thought. Underneath such self-destructive but unconscious motives, there was another more positive wish: to attract Father as a woman. Liz was even less aware of that need.

The Remaining Therapy and an
Excerpt from a Session

Soon after family therapy had started, the life history of the Williams family was unfolding and its fierce conflicts were making their first appearances in the therapeutic process. The therapist concluded early that the low point for Liz had already been passed. The family had helped itself, but there were more crises to weather.

Such notions had guided the therapist in his interpretations and in his conduct of the sessions. The family responded well with the memories, revelations, and clashes of opinion previously outlined. As the campaign against Father was closing in on him, he wavered between his desire to call off therapy and leave his family on the one hand and his feelings of sympathy and pity for the suffering and complaints of his three girls on the other. Eventually he grew more and more surprised at what he had missed about their feelings and thoughts through the years. Mother impressed him the most as she mediated between him and Jean and Liz, and he seemed to develop new, tender feelings for her. At one point he compared her to his sister and professed that he was sure he wanted no one like his sister (as he had repeatedly been accused of). Anna (Mother) was just right for him, she merely required a different approach, a different kind of attention, but he had failed her in that respect. Mother assured Father that he had not failed her very much, or rather that if he did, she understood. She had been used to neglect at home (in her family of origin).

What follows is an excerpt of a verbatim account of a session. As before, the thoughts of the therapist are spelled out in the right column:

Mother: Dad always came first. He got the best meat, the choicest fruit, first options on clothes, living space, and vacations. Even from my birthday cake he picked the best pieces. He snatched them when I was not looking. Or he challenged me to a game of cards or checkers—games, which he always won and cashed the stakes.

Mother's father sounds like a spoiled child all right.

Jean: Why didn't you protest? Or scream?

Jean wouldn't have tolerated that.

Mother: I was not even supposed to cry. Ma would hush me up or even hold my mouth shut so that Dad wouldn't hear me. Girls were not supposed to have complaints. They were for men to express. Sometimes I felt my father had to be treated like a little boy.

Liz: He has changed.

Jean: I remember him as kindly. He was available when we were there and had things that needed fixing. He always fixed them.

Mother's father is all right now, it seems.

Mother: He was more considerate of you than he ever was of me. He has been a better grandfather than a father. What's more, work never meant as much to him as it did to your father. Being a breadwinner was not important to him, and when we married I got next to nothing from him. If it hadn't been for Ma, we would have been without furniture for several months. Everything else that we have your father has earned himself, and when you marry one day, he has some money saved for you. He does not want you to start married life as the paupers we were. I didn't mind then. I thought love was all. Soon I had to change my mind. If it hadn't been for the early support of your father's parents, we would have starved.

As a grandfather, yes. It's at least something, but there is not much left for Mother when she was growing up. There was no help from her father when Mother got married.

Father (smiling): But love wasn't all . . . .

Shep (Father) is a good boy now.

Liz: I don't need any money. I don't want to marry.

Liz is bristling but not too severely.

Jean: I do. Some day.

Liz: Your stupid, ugly Peter?

Liz is jealous of Peter?

Jean: Not necessarily, but some day I want to have a family of my own.

What a calm reply by Jean.

Liz: Would I get the money even if I don't marry?

An appropriate, realistic question.

Mother (looking to Father): Marriage is not a condition, is it?

Mother, the kind mediator, as often before.

Father: It is not. When two people marry they need a little allowance, to be sure, but if a person wants to go on a long trip or to start a work project, money is important to have, too.

Father shows tolerance but not enough. He slips in his own values.

Liz: I don't want to start a work project. I don't want to go on a trip. I don't want to be shoved out of the house. I don't want to stay home either. I don't want to marry. Boys are disgusting.

Liz rejects external control; she still dreads it, especially from Father.

Jean: If you meet the right boy, it can be great.

A generous response by Jean.

Liz: You are a sucker for boys. They don't impress me. They all want the same. They want to lay you. They want to screw you, (screaming) but I dont want to be touched. I'll spit at them.

Liz cannot accept it yet. She is getting quite angry. She wants touching badly, but is afraid of boys.

Jean (after a short pause): You wouldn't at just one, would you?

Liz: Yes, I would. They are abominable. I detest them.

Jean: That will pass. Don't let them do anything to you that you don't like.

Another good, older sister advice.

Liz: You are crazy about hugs, I know. You would stay snuggled up to someone like Peter forever. I know. What's the point? How dumb can you get?

Liz hates Jean's relationship with Peter.

Therapist: Liz and Jean apparently disagree about contacts with boys. Is there someone, about whom you disagree completely? On the other hand, is there someone about whom you are in agreement?

Let us get down to some facts and actual experiences.

Jean (after a while): Liz doesn't like Peter at all.

Jean senses Liz's focus.

Liz: They should not hug and kiss each other in public.

Liz doesn't want to be tempted or provoked.

Jean: There isn't any hugging and kissing in public. You'd have to be a peeping Tom to catch us.

Jean retaliates a little.

Liz: Look at the pictures in your room. All those stupid couples wound up in each other with blissfully closed eyes. Who needs them? Do you look at them when you are alone?

(The pictures are drawings by Jean). Liz is very curious about what Jean does, thinks, and feels.

Liz: I rarely do.

Therapist (after looking around and at the daughters): Is there someone about whom you are in agreement? A male person who is not disgusting?

Let us try to focus on another example, perhaps a fatherly person.

Jean (after some thinking): Mr. Gladwell?

Liz: No.

Jean: Didn't you praise him for his fairness?

Liz: He reads test papers carefully. He is an interested teacher.

Mr. Gladwell seems to be a fatherly person to Liz.

Therapist: A touchable teacher?

Let us lead Liz a little more.

Liz: Heavens no.

Jean: You said he was attractive.

Liz: I never said anything like that. . . .

Liz denies any amorous interest.

Therapist: How about your parents? Are they touchable people?

Let us sound out Liz's tender needs for Father.

Liz: They are parents. That's another story.

Therapist: Are they? Do the daughters enjoy their hugs?

Jean: I don't mind.

Liz: That's another story. Mother is a woman. And Father doesn't care. He wants me to be out of the house.

Since Father does not care, Liz implies, I must have no tender feelings for him whatever.

Mother: He loves you. He is very concerned. You know that . . . .

Mother, the kind mediator again.

After a long pause Liz brought up her wish to get a second dog, something that had come up in therapy before and had been a subject of discussion in the Williams family for more than a year. Liz had wanted her own dog. The parents argued that Arco was her dog. If she paid less attention to him, as she had, Arco could not be blamed for trying to

attach himself to other family members, too. There was some
more talk about teachers and conversations Mother had with
them on parents' day and a resolution that on next parents'
day Father should come.

What the therapist had been steering toward, however,
was how Liz felt about physical contact with her father. It
came out two sessions later when, incidentally, he had to
skip the meeting for professional reasons — a good one, they
all agreed — that the only man Liz could imagine going to bed
with was her father. That left Mother and Jean dumb-
founded for a while, but the therapist did not flinch. After a
pause (to give the girls and Mother time to respond if they
wanted to), he commented that in spite of many, on-going
complaints and attacks on Father, he was a very important
and basically trustworthy person to her. Liz replied that he
was not trustworthy because he did not care about her, but
he was the only man she found physically not detestable.

After another pause Mother and Jean engaged in a
dialogue about attractive and unattractive men. Jean volunteered that her first sexual experiences were unpleasant
indeed. She had believed she had to accommodate her
boyfriend regardless of how she felt herself. She has since
come a long way, she claimed. It's a matter of waiting for the
boy you really like, and there is much more to it than mere
physical attraction.

"How do you know whether you really like a boy," Liz
asked. After pausing, Mother added that it takes time and
the best thing to do is to see more than one young man at a
time. "Then, after dating for a while, you become more
confident of your choice. If the feelings are mutual, you can
pursue the relationship further," her mother continued. Jean
seemed to agree with the mother and told Liz of an early
friendship. Liz was not interested but wondered about Peter,
Jean's current friend. Liz was surprised to learn that although this was a love relationship, Jean was not sure it

would last. Liz wondered: "If you love, don't you love forever?"

It was obvious that even now, while family therapy was going on, a good deal of the work and change was accomplished outside the therapeutic sessions, albeit in spurts and unpredictably. The family therapist, a man of the classical school, spent part of the time, sometimes even a major portion of the sessions on checking inconspicuously what had happened in between. Needless to say, some of the most essential interpersonal processes remained undiscussed, although an experienced therapist could detect what they were. It was obvious to the therapist that Liz was in a process of revising her image of Father. She got thoughtful help from family members, something family therapists cannot always count on. Although she was moved by the discussion and her own expression of feelings, Liz was neither forced to reveal herself further nor to tell how she felt now nor to accept the family's advice. Jean and Mother were sharing their experiences with each other, and Liz was able to listen in if she cared to, which she did, more and more often.

Once Liz's intensive preoccupation with her father was out in the open and had not stirred up the havoc that Liz might unconsciously have anticipated, she became a bit freer to venture out to other men, and one obvious person was the therapist, a person approximately of her father's age. The therapist suspected that Liz unconsciously wanted most of all to rant and rave against her father or, if it made no impression on him, against herself. If Father was truly responsive to her, she felt he would listen to her and hold and comfort her, just as her mother had done with her. If Liz's anger was hard to contain, the therapist hoped her father would still hold her, with gentle force, and prevent her from hitting, scratching, or biting him until her anger was spent or stilled. His restraint would allow her love to come through her hostility. Hopefully, if she could relent to more positive feelings toward him and if Father did not shrink from her display of them, she would be sure of his love as she probably once was in her childhood. The reestablishment of trust would enable her to branch out to other males.

The therapist was certain that some of this development might occur vicariously in feelings expressed toward himself. He had been and continued to be prepared for her occasional abuse and aggression as well as for some probing of his concern for her.

Father and Mother had learned quite a few things about each other and their past relationship, and, fortunately, they were still learning. They felt closer and in greater harmony than they had for many years, Father conceded. As the therapist saw it, Father was, for the first time, making persistent effort to fuse his two roles: that of brother of a sister (but not as much the younger brother any longer) and that of older brother as his father had been (but not so much as sibling to only brothers). He became more considerate and protective of his wife. In that way he relieved her of the pressure to be an older sister (the role her parents presumably had wanted her to assume and to which she had dutifully responded) and permitted her to be more like an only child or even a younger sister (of a sister, like her mother).

Jean stepped in as the older sister she, in fact, was. She turned out to be quite mature for her age and was able to pull together with her parents in their efforts to change and to deal positively with Liz. Even her own communications with Liz improved and became much more acceptable to Liz than they had been for a long time. Liz learned that she did not always have to out-rival and outdo Jean. Occasionally, Jean could do nurturing things for her as well, and Jean did not wait for any special favors in return for them, Liz felt.

Arco, the family pet, could have come along to family therapy if the family had insisted, but when it was suggested one day, Liz refused to have him join. The others did not oppose her wishes, but they never inquired about the reasons for her refusal. The therapist thought that it was possibly out of a sense of failure that Liz had been feeling most intensely at that time. Liz implied that she was afraid that in the eyes of the therapist she was not fit to care for even a dog. At the time, though, her interest in boys was budding and she felt confident, even without immediate proofs of success, of her ability to attract boys; and that achievement would be more worthy of someone's notice than any skill in training a dog.

Family therapy went on for a while, the intervals became greater and eventually it was resolved in session that therapy should end. To everybody's surprise Liz flung her arms around the therapist's neck, buried her face briefly on his shoulder, and left a tear there. It was agreed that any one of the Williams family or all of them could come again, should the need arise.

Some Concluding Remarks

At this point readers may want to check the theoretical portrait or blind diagnosis the therapist had offered based on only skeleton facts about the Williams family. The case report fleshed out the diagnosis and apparently confirmed a number of conjectures. Readers can best judge for themselves the extent of their accuracy.

What transpired in this case history, moreover, is the attitude with which the therapist viewed his own reasoning. He did not regard it as truth. Rather his reasoning is a sorting out of possibilities and ordering them according to their probabilities. It is an attempt to find the basic wishes, tendencies, and motives of the persons involved and the ways such tendencies developed and clashed with the others in the family. As the family drama unfolds and the stakes and fortunes of each member become more apparent, the therapist is prepared to discard some of his conjectures and modify a few others.

Does it pay then for the therapist to think through and diagnose the assumptions drawn from the questionnaire or other information received prior to therapy? Shouldn't he rather just follow his intuitions? Should he concentrate on only feeling and leave out the details about social context, life situation, and family history that are hard to disentangle or remember? The answer to the first question is yes, to the second a qualified yes, and to the third a clear no. A deeper look at these questions is required.

Does it pay for the therapist to reason beforehand and as therapy moves on? It is useful for the therapist to reflect on the ways he thinks about his patients at any stage throughout their psychotherapy. In the beginning of a therapist's career as a practitioner, he needs a sounding board, a colleague, a team, or a supervisor. As he becomes more experienced, he can record his evaluations on paper or merely in his mind. He needs to scrutinize his reasoning processes in order to evaluate his understanding of his patients. Expectations and anticipations of content or patient behavior, both in real life and in psychotherapy, form the basis of the therapist's reasoning, and they can turn out to be valid or not. If they are wrong, he needs to reevaluate his thinking. In this process of consistent, honest evaluation the therapist's thinking will become clearer, more stringent, and acute. If he neglects this process, he will be less aware of expectations that come true in the course of therapy and those that don't. He learns less about the validity of his own thinking and his growth as a therapist.

Should the therapist follow his intuitions? The therapist cannot conduct therapy other than intuitively, spontaneously, and naturally, but he will have to assess the accuracy of his intuitions. To some extent this assessment of intuitions is always going on vis-à-vis his reasoning and conjectures, and in that process he usually finds himself articulating those conjectures. However, if he is disinterested in his intuitions or simply forgets them, he will not learn as much as he could about his patients or about himself as a therapist. Over time he may not improve enough to meet his own professional needs or the therapeutic needs of his patients.

Should the therapist ignore social context, life situation, and family history? If a therapist seriously concentrates only on the patients' feelings, he will soon find out that his patients won't let him. They themselves mix in the minutia of their living conditions both present and past with their feelings about people who are important in their lives. They seem to sense that feelings are unintelligible except as responses to realities, and although it is true that realities have to be perceived in order to become effective, the patients' perceptions of reality cannot be ignored. This includes *misperceptions*—even they have at least some basis in reality, often in a reality of the patients' past. Therefore, if a therapist insists on hearing about just feelings, patients may simply walk out on him before long.

However the problem remains: how does the therapist keep track of the social context, the family background, and family history in which a patient has grown up. Taking notes during the therapeutic session can be helpful if it does not distract the therapist and the patients permit it. Otherwise, he should make notes as soon after the session as possible. This may take a little time, but in fairness to his patients the therapist should have that time anyway before he sees the next patient. The therapist may use audio- or videotapes if the patients do not object. Yet he would still need his notes, since reviewing the tapes might take as much time as a therapeutic session. Reviewing his notes, however, even at a later time, will take only minutes.

The reader may ask whether this is too much ado about psychotherapy. Not if the therapist wants to keep a record of what he has done, and without some record not even he will know with certainty what that was. He may retain the experience and the expertise to be sure, but the details will slowly disappear in a haze. In the long run even his expertise may suffer.

5

THE COMPLEX TASK
OF THE
FAMILY THERAPIST

PSYCHOTHERAPY IN GENERAL

A therapeutic relationship is neither one of nurture and care, nor one of competition or ordinary partnership.* In an ordinary partnership, common interests have been recognized by the partners as more valuable for each of them than the pursuit of their conflicting interests. A therapeutic relationship is no love relationship, either. A love relationship could be called a comprehensive, special-case partnership. A therapeutic relationship may assume any of these features for periods of time, but in essence it is something else.

Some say, psychotherapy starts with a contract. Others

---

*"The Complex Task of the Family Therapist" originally appeared as a lecture given at the Family Therapy Symposium of Georgetown University, Washington, D.C., on October 21, 1984.

call it an alliance. However, it is not like ordinary contracts. It is like no other type of alliance. It requires a selfless sympathy for the needs of patients—for their more trivial needs as well as the more crucial ones, and their destructive needs as much as their highest aspirations. The patients' love-interests and fulfillment should not make us therapists envious or jealous, nor should their hatred and rage arouse in us retaliation or fear. The patients' fears, anxieties, and sorrows should not disturb us. We should not become anxious or helpless ourselves or be tempted to stir up optimism in the patients, nor should we become impatient with their sadness. An essential step in achieving a higher level of therapy is the experience of psychotherapy itself. The therapist should know himself rather well, and the best guarantee for that knowledge in the eyes of those who have assumed the responsibility of training is therapeutic self-exploration under the guidance of a training therapist.

What's more of a problem is the claim that no other forms of self-exploration are acceptable. Another problem is the built-in but extrinsic reward for this particular form of self-exploration, which is admission to further training and eventual membership in the organization with permission to practice psychotherapy. Some observers suspect that this extrinsic reward on self-exploration may generate an intrinsic bias for a club's special school of therapy and for an attitude of awe that the ordinary patient is supposed to assume toward this therapy and the therapist. Yet, there is no a priori reason for awe. The ordinary patient, in fact, is the truer judge of a therapist's merits. When he finds that therapy is helping him, he is testing its intrinsic value. When he cannot endure it, at least in the long run, it is no good for the patient.

The main purpose of all this self-exploration is to help the would-be therapist to know himself and his feelings, needs, and conflicts better than before in order to resolve most of his conflicts and to fulfill his hopes and wishes in everyday life so that they will no longer interfere with his observations of others and with his therapeutic interactions.

The second essential step for a therapist-in-training is to conduct several psychotherapies under supervision of more than one seasoned therapist. This step is considered the real training in psychotherapy. Communication with the supervisor about the conduct of psychotherapy ranges from mental or written notes to playing audio- and videotapes of the sessions. Psychologically, it is concerned with the candidate-therapist's ability to observe the patient and understand his perceptions, feelings, needs, motives, and communications, to think along the patient's point of view, and to create a picture in his own mind of the patient's life history, of the significant persons in the patient's life, and of the patient himself as a person. The subtle discourse between supervisor and candidate of psychotherapy focuses on the candidate's psychotherapeutic interventions. The goal of this discourse is a modest one: to reduce in the candidate the likelihood of misperceptions and misinterpretations of the patient's views, feelings, thoughts, needs, and reality, and thereby to improve the candidate's therapeutic interventions. Technically speaking, one could say the goal is the gradual elimination of the candidate-therapist's tendencies of countertransference, that is, of his tendencies to misunderstand the patient and his situation in light of the therapist's own problems and conflicts.

The third precaution is for the candidate-therapist or graduate therapist to have come to terms with his own life situation. If at all possible, he or she should have achieved in real life many of his aspired goals. Ordinarily, this includes a partner for life, a home, children. His basic survival needs must be satisfied. Feeling persistently tempted by a patient should be a reason for the therapist to look for additional supervision or therapy or to send the patient to someone else. Actively seducing a patient or giving in to a patient's advances is one of a therapist's cardinal sins. Due to the uniqueness of the therapeutic situation, it requires sanctions. The patient's true interests must be protected.

WHAT MAKES IT PSYCHOTHERAPY?

What makes the therapeutic situation so unique? Why has it puzzled some psychotherapists to the point of questioning whether therapy can be done at all? To begin with, the therapist offers help in self-help. He listens attentively and sympathetically and empathizes with the patient. He helps the patient to express his wishes and thoughts in the order that the patient chooses. The therapist takes the liberty, however, of coming back to the topics that the patient has broached when the patient pauses. The therapist comments and interprets the patient's messages and communications, but he does not tell him what to do. He offers no advice. He does not teach the patient anything and does not help him materially. He helps the patient, though, to muster *his own* advice, to utilize his own experiences, and to draw on his own resources better than he or she did before.

This, at least, is classical psychotherapy. Some therapists think they may depart from it after a while and under certain circumstances, but even they will start out in that fashion until they have learned enough about the patient to dare to assume direction and take shortcuts. Those who depart from classical psychotherapy right from the start of treatment may not even be true therapists. Perhaps there is no need for them to be, but then they do not merit the name either.

Psychotherapy is the recapturing of some opportunities for satisfaction and fulfillment that a patient believes he has lost—and often has—and the pursuing of those old or similar, more realizable goals. Some opportunities may continue to be unavailable to the patient even after treatment, but then the hunger for them and the pain or guilt of longing can be softened. Better ways of relinquishing these goals can be acquired. The therapist follows the patient in his free flow of memories, fantasies, wishes, and affects whether they concern the past or the present, subjective experiences or objective events. Nearly all of them concern people—people, who are sometimes loved, sometimes hated, sometimes feared, sometimes mourned. The order in which the patient moves through these themes, the way he switches back and forth from person to person in his life, is essentially spontaneous. This odyssey, exactly, is what the patient will have to do eventually in order to increase his potential in reality, to become more courageous, freer, and more successful in his pursuit of happiness; of happiness that may include other people's happiness and that of his own children who are likely to exceed his own lifespan.

The therapist follows the patient's every meandering expression of thought and feeling. With his questions, cautious comments, and even more cautious interpretations the therapist accompanies the patient responsively and gently. At the same time, the therapist is not directly involved. He is not a member of the patient's family, not a friend, nor a party to his daily chores and struggles, although during the therapeutic sessions the patient is often trying unconsciously to draw him into everything.

The therapist is always the potential "other," sometimes like a mother, a teacher, an uncle, a brother, a son or daughter, a friend, or even a lover. Yet, his assuming actively any of these roles in the therapeutic relationship would terminate classical therapy and would be quite unfair to the patient, no matter how urgently the patient might want this.

A personal friendship between therapist and patient

would be professionally tolerable only after psychotherapy has been terminated and a period of time gone by without any contact between the two, which is optimally at least as long a time as the psychotherapy. Otherwise, the therapist could not be sure that he has not abused the patient's emotional dependence on him. That emotional dependence is a temporary but integral part of psychotherapy and makes the patient quite vulnerable for a time. It should never, never be used to satisfy any of the therapist's personal needs or of his needs toward the patient.

Following the patient's rambles and meanders of the mind closely and understandingly is probably the core of the therapeutic process. The patient does not get to know the therapist as a person. The therapist is self-effacing. Not necessarily in his private life, to be sure, although some therapists tend to be "therapeutic" even at home and with their children. That can be a grave mistake. No, the therapist is self-effacing in the sense of empathy and identification with the patient. His own self is in the background. He feels and thinks with the patient. He responds to the patient with greater clarity, equanimity, and objectivity than the patient can. The patient is all engrossed in and engulfed by his life context and life history and all the people in it. The therapist is not. He looks over the patient's shoulder. He participates in the patient's emotions and longings and conflicts to the extent that the patient lets him in. If all goes well, the patient does let him in more and more.

In contrast to what the patient may feel about the therapist, the therapist is a kind of nonperson to the patient. Hence, the therapist can be all persons that matter in the patient's life. The therapist can even be the patient himself. He can take each and every part of the patient, that of a hopeful child, a fighting or scared adult, a parent or a loving dreamer, and observe it with the clarity, equanimity, and objectivity of the outsider who has entered the mind of the patient temporarily. This observation is based on what the patient tells him and what he, the therapist, can conjecture. He can retain his calm because he has not really met the patient's family and friends; he is none of them, and he is not permanently stranded in the patient's life.

What the patients can ultimately learn from the therapist and what they can take home after therapy has ended is to handle their own feelings, problems, and conflicts the way the therapist has been handling them during treatment. Although the therapist reveals nothing about himself, at least he does reveal how he conducts a dialogue with the patient. After treatment has ended, the patient can talk to himself with the same consideration the therapist expressed to him. That respectful concern is the part of the therapist that the patient can take home, no matter how elusive he has appeared to the patient during therapy.

FAMILY THERAPY

In the preceding sections I have been talking only about individual therapy, and as the reader knows, it is a rather complicated affair. How much more complicated must it be to conduct group therapy or family therapy. Whereas classical group therapy—with patients not knowing each other prior to therapy and seeing each other only in the group sessions—is somewhat like a multiple of individual therapy, family therapy is a category in and of itself with respect to complexity. There are countless chances for pitfalls.

Who would be crazy enough to think that he can help a group help itself that has lived together for many years with growing and ever changing connections with the larger world? The family members are of different ages and sexes and have very different abilities and powers. They are bonded to each other in complex ways by emotions, attitudes, interests, and conflicts, and they interact physically and verbally in a multitude of ways. They engage in alliances of various kinds and combinations for a variety of reasons. Some of these alliances may be as old as some of the family members involved; others may have been formed recently. When such a family decides they need help and a family therapist is selected, he is often expected to do his job in a few sessions, and he cannot be sure whether they will even let him get a foot in the door.

Therapeutic interactions between people occur in everyday life. They probably occur in great number, but they cannot be counted on and often helpful advice is ignored. There is even professional psychotherapeutic help that can be had in a short time, sometimes in a single session, or in just a few. The efficacy of such sporadic psychotherapy should not be underestimated. Sometimes help on a particular issue is all a person needs. After that, he can help himself without a therapeutic participant.

If a family in need is looking for help of that kind, for help on a particular issue, for insight and change of attitude within the family in some particular respect, then the family can probably be accommodated by a family therapist. The trouble is that even in individual therapy a particular issue is almost never the only problem involved, and this finding is even more true of a family in search of help (Bowen 1959, 1978).

If individual therapy may actually be interminable (Freud 1937) and merely has to be stopped at some point for practical reasons, family therapists, too, can live with such a state of affairs. In fact, more than the individual therapist he will have to. Family life usually is in rapid progress or acute turmoil when family therapy is sought. In individual and group therapy of adults, even in therapy of childless couples, the patients have usually left the family of origin.

Although they still carry their family members within themselves, the patients' interactions with them have diminished.

Hence, the amount of psychotherapeutic work, the degree of inner change, and even the closeness to something like the completion of treatment can be appraised more easily in individual therapy than it can in family therapy. In individual therapy, for example, the end of treatment may be approaching when the patient's comments and interpretations about himself have become similar to those of his therapist. He has identified with the therapist and can more or less do without him.

Because of the turbulence of daily life, the irrepressible long-term development, and the number of people involved, appraising therapeutic progress in family therapy is much more of a problem.

The family therapist would have to be even more cautious and attentive, more sympathetic and empathic at first than any other therapist. Otherwise, he will be unable to uncover what's on their minds. On the other hand, dealing with an ongoing family life, its struggles and recurring changes, demands that his interpretations and his behavior have more impact than those of any other type of therapist. He will have to track every family member, almost like a dog, in their feelings, wishes, and thoughts. He will have to prove to each of them that he understands them, possibly better than all other family members, at least on certain issues. And he will have to impress more in those ways than the ordinary therapist does impress his patients. That is how he can hope to do something toward the better integration of the family members into one family life, or at least into a more coherent one.

This is a tall order. Yet, family therapy does not call for a megalomanic, a bluff, or an exhibitionist. The family therapist should say what he sees and hears clearly, calmly, and objectively, but he should remain in the background as a person. The family should not take home to mull over between sessions the image of a boisterous father, an ever-condoning mother, a dictator, an entertainer, an impervious fighter for the children, or a ranting prophet. They will anyway. They take home all sorts of things of their own making and imagination, but the family therapist should not literally have deliberately or impulsively enacted any of these roles. At least not for a while.

If the family therapist can engage the family members in an exchange among themselves, if by his own interventions he can accentuate, clarify, or interpret what each family member or the family group is trying to convey, and if he can articulate their problems and conflicts, and encourage them to discuss solutions—all in such a manner that they do not remember him but rather their own contributions to therapy—he has, in the long run, done them a good service. Even if the therapist's interpretations are apt and beautifully phrased, so well perhaps that none of the family members would ever have made them, they should feel that they could have. The phrasing was what they meant or might feel, and what is meant is what matters.

The minimal goal of therapy is a continuation of the kind of discussion and exchange among the family members at home that they have experienced during therapy sessions. They notice that other family members want to say something and, occasionally, they now let them. They don't interrupt them; rather, they try to understand. If they get to know each other better that way, if they empathize a little more with what the others are longing and striving for, and if they can listen, at least occasionally, without any ulterior motive, just as a participant in the other person's mind, the family may have benefited even beyond minimal expectations.

There would be no harm in family members' sounding

at home somewhat like the family therapist on occasion, perhaps even in being ridiculed for doing so. The scoffers may have a memory of how it could be done better. This is how they can and do take the family therapist into their home. Needless to say, that the number of family members who can identify with the family therapist in this way and the variety of issues and roles that they bring up in the process is usually revealing something about the therapist's conduct of family therapy. If only one member of the family can enact the therapist's role at home and if it is always the same role, say, a bully or a chronic masochist, the family therapist probably has not yet served the family very well.

PRECAUTIONS FOR THE FAMILY THERAPIST CANDIDATE

What precautions have the various schools in the family therapy movement more or less agreed upon in order to produce adequate family therapists? If they have not outright adopted the precautions of individual psychotherapy, they have adopted at least analogs. One is self-exploration as exploration of one's own family background. Understanding yourself is understanding your family history, the characters that contributed to it, your present family life, and yourself as a product and agent of the family process. This can be done in various ways; family therapy, group therapy, and even individual therapy being among the preferred methods.

Another precaution is conducting family therapy under supervision. Here, group therapy and family therapy have a decisive advantage over individual therapy: The candidate-therapist can be an observer of an experienced group or family therapist. He can be his co-therapist. He can even ask his supervisor to attend his, the candidate's, group or family therapy as a co-therapist. This is like swimming in a swimming-pool with a companion who is used to the open waters. The experience shows and can be perceived by the candidate-therapist.

The third precaution is for the candidate or graduate family therapist to have come to terms with his own life. He should have his own family, or at least strongly want one. A person who thinks little of family life or is even determined to never have a family himself or herself should probably shift their focus to another type of therapy. Moreover, a future family therapist should also have come to terms with his own family. This process began during his self-exploration via his family background, to be sure, but his efforts should be uninterrupted. The family therapist ought to be in a dialogue with his or her immediate family as well as with the family of origin. How can a therapist expect a patient's family to undertake such things if he doesn't do them himself.

THE PSYCHOTHERAPIST AT WORK

A family therapist may have studied and come to terms with his family of origin and may have founded his own family and be getting along reasonably well. He may be practicing family therapy under supervision, or alone, or even as a supervisor and teacher. He knows himself and he knows how to do therapy in many kinds of circumstances. Yet, with all this training and work, he may still have retained certain idiosyncrasies or tendencies of countertransference that will affect his conduct of therapy. Often, they may be negligible, but sometimes they can amount to serious handicaps. Let me illustrate a few.

Allow me first to mention the regional, ethnic, religious, socioeconomic, or language differences between therapist and patient. Obviously they matter. If there are great discrepancies between therapist and patient, they can be an obstacle to useful therapy. This is particularly true, if therapist and patient do not speak a common language. If they do, however, the therapist owes his patient or his family in treatment all concessions he can muster. He should speak their language, pick up their idiom, use their expressions rather than his own, and be able to adopt their viewpoints.

Let us compare therapist and patient in a few more elementary social aspects. What if a family therapist has come from an intact and happy family and everything in his life went smoothly. One might wonder, why he chose to be a family therapist to begin with and, more significantly, whether he can understand those in trouble. The question remains, can a person from such a background understand those in trouble, those who have suffered losses in their families, those who have seen hell from the surviving members? He will have to struggle. Inversely, how can a family therapist who has had very hard times in his life understand a family who seems to be on top of the world and has just one minor problem: The husband wants to retain both his wife and his lover.

A therapist and individual patient of opposite sex encourages love-related topics in the patient's memories, fantasies, and transference behavior a little more at first than usual (Toman 1961). Psychotherapy starts moving sooner, but may be a bit harder to terminate. Therapist and patient who are the same sex have a relationship that is somewhat more conducive to topics of contest and status. The patient more quickly identifies with the therapist, therefore, initially psychotherapy is slower, but its eventual termination is a bit easier on the patient.

A large age difference between therapist and patient tends to activate parent–child or teacher–student relationships in therapy and in transference onto the therapist. Little or no age difference between the two is more conducive to peer relationships and feelings and conflicts that originate in sibling relationships. A therapist who is substantially younger than his patient may evoke in him parental feelings toward the therapist, and topics of caretaking, responsibility, and possibly some expressions of distrust may well form an undercurrent in the relationship.

Therapists who are oldest siblings tend to overprotect and overcontrol their patients. Therapists who are youngest siblings are likely to undercontrol, to take greater chances, to act on impulse and intuition, and sometimes to become competitive with their patients. Therapists who are from middle sibling positions are likely to do neither. Early on, they have had practice in responding in more than one way at home and toward people. Their own identity, or rather, lack of it, may distract them a little. They may perceive identity struggles in patients where there aren't any. On the other hand, therapists who are from single-child families are likely to focus on a patient's individuality and his relationships to parents and authority figures more than on other relationships. The therapist may even long for parental attention and admiration from the patient. Therapists who had opposite-sex siblings are more at ease in psychotherapy with love-related problems; those who had only same-sex siblings feel more comfortable dealing rather with problems of work, achievement, competition, cooperation, and power.

Therapists who have suffered losses of family members are often more sensitive to fears of loss in their patients and to possible effects of those losses on patients than are those who have never experienced such loss. In some instances, however, they unduly ignore the loss. They respond as if from within a shell. Occasionally, they feel that compared to what they had to cope with themselves, the patient's losses are a trifle. "You should know my suffering," they may sometimes feel tempted to tell a patient.

If therapists have never been exposed to losses of family members, they are likely to underestimate the effects of those losses—permanent, temporary, and partial losses—that their patients have suffered. Some of the deep or deeply covered listlessness and dependency needs of such patients escape them. If these patients have to reexperience their grief with the support of the therapist in order to ultimately overcome it, they may not get it from therapists who have been too blissfully happy or lucky in their early lives.

This is, among other things, why we assume that some exposure in his own life to loss of dear ones, or at least to conflict involving threat of loss, is beneficial for a therapist. If he had no such exposure, he may never develop even the wish to help those who are suffering. On the other hand, if he had too much exposure, if the losses had occurred too early in his life and had deeply traumatic consequences, he may still develop the wish to help others, but his own need for help might be too great. His capacity to conduct therapy may well be diminished.

THE FAMILY THERAPIST AT WORK

Although the preceding problems stem from issues related to individual therapy, they are all equally applicable to group therapy and family therapy, only in much more complicated ways. A family therapist responds to each family member *interactively*, which may include, for example, the following: He feels slightly irritated by the somewhat pompous father and notices a fleeting urge to put the man in his place. (Hopefully, he won't.) He finds the mother a bit anxious, attractive, and worthy of a more caring husband. The daughter impresses him as a scrawny girl in early puberty who is wearing a skirt but looks as though she prefers jeans, and perhaps, wishes she were a boy. She has a very pretty face, but a sullen look. The son of 7 can do no wrong in the father's eyes, it seems. He is sure of himself, too sure perhaps. He is probably used to being the center of attention. In spite of this arrogance he seems to be a delightful boy, the therapist notes.

As the example shows, while the therapist is interacting with each family member, he is also *identifying* with each of them. His impressions seem to indicate that he is perhaps identifying the least with the father, although he is a father himself. He does not want to be that kind of father. Yet if the therapist tried to substitute for any family member, the most likely assignment would be the father's. If the therapist were a woman, mother and therapist would more likely be rivals for the family's attention.

The therapist is also responding to, and identifying with, the family as a group. Our therapist has his family of origin—the basis of his experiences of family life, even though he has looked into the family lives among relatives and friends, too. What may be of greater immediate consequence to therapy, are the many families that he has seen as a therapist. They were families of various configurations, we might assume, and hopefully the diversity should have helped him to keep his personal bias in check. The therapist I have in mind and who happens to be seeing the Smith family is a father, has a wife and a son of 19, but his marriage is not entirely in order. He has a woman friend, a divorcee, and his wife has a married man for a lover who does not want to divorce his wife. He is keeping his affair a secret from his wife. The therapist's son has dropped out of school and wants to become a painter or a conductor, but has not made a concerted effort toward his goal for the last two years.

The impaired family circumstances just described cannot be an asset to conducting therapy. Will such a therapist think that his patient family's life need not be too satisfying either? Or will he perhaps try to make up for his own deficiencies by intemperate offers to help? Will he take excessive interest in the family's problems in order to protect the patient's family from a fate like his own?

Let me briefly describe what the first sessions of therapy revealed about the family and where the therapist may have had some initial difficulties. The designated patient in the Smith family was the 14-year-old girl Jenny who hated boys and had an eating problem. She claimed she was interested in school, but lately she had not performed well. Her little brother, Bob, was a nuisance to her although she did not dare to say so. As it turned out, Bob pestered her with silly questions about her body. Bob had also molested little girls in school, Mrs. Smith admitted with some discomfort, but Mr. Smith laughed it off. The therapist's initial impression, that the boy could do no wrong, bore him out, it appeared.

Mr. Smith worked in the sales department of a medium-sized company and had a way with the ladies. He insisted that his behavior was part of business and that Mrs. Smith would simply have to understand. Mrs. Smith now seemed resigned but had been rather unhappy for years. Her daughter served as her confidante. The two women seemed to have agreed that men are little boys that cannot be trusted, and they always want sex. Whereas Mrs. Smith had been able to feel basically motherly toward her son and her husband, Jenny resented such feelings toward them furiously.

Those attitudes extended to the therapist. Mrs. Smith was almost flirting with the therapist to the point of making Mr. Smith quite jealous of him. Jenny, in contrast, bristled whenever the therapist tried to convey that he was on Jenny's side and understood her feelings. She did not want to be touched by anybody, not even by sympathy. The therapist recalled in retrospect that he had felt warmly and sympathetically toward Mrs. Smith, but somewhat tempted by the fantasy of being the man who would awaken the woman in Jenny. A Lolita complex of the therapist? He never succumbed, though.

Mr. Smith discovered that he had not given a damn about what men thought of him, although his own father had been an exacting person who had wanted him to excel in school. In the course of the sessions he and Bob seemed to try to resolve in their minds that men did indeed matter in this world and that they, Mr. Smith and Bob, had not lived up to their potential at work and in school. More important perhaps, Father and Bob, respectively, began to wonder what Mother thought and felt. Eventually Jenny was included in these pangs of conscience, and father embarked on an involved apology, which he tried to address to Jenny in a roundabout way but actually expressed to his wife. It turned out that Mrs. Smith had lost her father when she was 12 and had suffered because of it. Her own mother, a somewhat pampered and childish woman, Mrs. Smith recalled, had grown into a quietly, strong person after her husband's death in an accident. She never remarried.

Under such an onslaught of attention and reparation by her husband and son, Mrs. Smith occasionally argued with a twinkle that they should not overdo it. Toward the end of treatment, Jenny could not help smiling at the therapist, her first and only one, when he had said in an argument over some boys in Jenny's class that, if Jenny had an interest in one of the boys she would not want to tell, and she would not want to be questioned, least of all by Bob.

There is more to tell, but let me briefly indicate how the family background data had been helpful in understanding their life together and how the therapist's own family background may have interacted with the patient family's background, beyond what I have already suggested.

Mr. Smith was the adored younger brother of two sisters. His sisters looked after him in his early life. Perhaps it was he, not his son, who could do no wrong. However, Mr. Smith's father had been an older brother of a brother. The relationship could have led to some discontent between him and Mr. Smith, also to somewhat less than successful attempts by Mr. Smith to identify with his father. Maybe, the therapist's original impression of Mr. Smith as a pompous man was an indication of such a failure or refusal to become like the father.

Mrs. Smith, the middle sister of an older sister and a younger brother in her family of origin, had often been asked to take care of her little brother, but her older sister outdid her at that task. Part of it may have been Mrs. Smith's own rivalry feelings toward her brother. After he was born, she was no longer the youngest. The situation did not improve for Mrs. Smith after her father died when she was only 12.

It seemed that Mr. Smith had married someone like the less important of his two sisters, and Mrs. Smith had been the less important sister in her own family. Unconsciously, that is, in some reminiscence of old jealousies of her older sister who could handle their youngest brother better than she, Mrs. Smith would only hesitatingly teach Jenny how to be motherly toward the little boy Bob. On the other hand, Jenny and Bob are seven years apart. That is a little too much to become close siblings anyway.

The *therapist* had been the younger brother of a brother, his wife the younger sister of a sister in their families of origin. He had not learned at home how to deal with peer girls, and his wife had not learned how to deal with peer boys. Both of them are youngest children and both are in need of leadership, we would assume.

This marriage would be considered to be an unfavorable match, all things being equal. True enough, they have only one child and seem to have quite a problem with him. They are tending toward separation.

Unfortunately perhaps, the therapist's lover is also a

The Smith Family

$$b(b)/m \, / \, / \, (ss)b \, / \, s_{14} \, b_7 \, / \, (s)s(b) \, / \, / \, f/m$$

Father's   Father   Mother   Mother's
parents   parents
                        Jenny Bob

The Therapist's Family

$$b(b)/m \, / \, / \, (b)b \, / \, b_{19} \, / \, (s)s \, / \, / \, f/m$$

therapist   wife

therapist's   son   wife's
parents   parents

Therapist's and his wife's *extramarital relations*

(b)b / *(s)s*   *b(ssb)* / (s)s

therapist   wife

---

younger sister of a sister, though ten years younger than his
wife.

The therapist's wife has done better in that respect. Her
lover is the older brother of two sisters and a brother.
However, he does not want to divorce his wife. Why? Many
reasons probably, none of which we ever truly discovered,
except one: the man's wife is a younger sister of two
brothers. That configuration would create a favorable match,
but why should he be looking for an extramarital relationship? Two possible reasons: his wife may be more loyal to
her brothers than he can tolerate; or his lover, the therapist's
wife, may be more impulsive, more competitive, more

exciting, and more appreciative of male leadership than his wife. He may like the challenge of a competitive woman.

Whatever the therapist had to offer to the females in the Smith family may not be based much on his own family background but perhaps on what he had learned later from conducting therapy with respect to women's wants and needs.

The therapist's family background was more congenial probably with the male part of the Smith family. The therapist, too, had an older brother of a brother for a father, just like Mr. Smith, and the therapist was outdone by his older brother in becoming like his father. However, he may have been a more pleasant younger brother to his father than was his father's brother. And it was, after all, a man's world—a world of competition, work, and achievement and loyalty to men, so they felt. That is what the therapist may have been able to sensitize Mr. Smith and Bob to. Not by telling them about his own experiences, to be sure, but by spotting more readily than Mr. Smith and Bob could themselves some of those ambitious and competitive implications in their own lives. In accordance with his father's aspirations for him, Mr. Smith's relationship with his father may have improved, and the existence of male peers become more acceptable to both, Mr. Smith and Bob. It dawned on them that competition for females is something that can be won through courtship, that is, by being considerate of and sensitive to women and their needs, not by taking them for granted and being abusive.

CONCLUDING REMARKS

We have once more gone over the process of psychotherapy and family therapy, over the therapist's predicaments, problems, skills, goals, and hopes. A very brief discussion of a third case of family therapy culminated in a sketch of interacting family backgrounds in the discourse between patient and therapist. In this book it is no more than a hint. In classical family therapy, however, it is perhaps the most intricate of the complexities of treatment, albeit no explicit subject of the therapeutic exchange. It is something that the classical family therapist usually tries to handle backstage, mostly with his colleagues, in his team conferences, or with his therapeutic supervisor—sometimes even with his old training therapist. If he does that, and conscientiously so, his patients will ultimately benefit.

REFERENCES

Ackerman, N. W. (1958). *Psychodynamics of Family Life.* New York: Basic Books.

――― (1966). *Treating the Troubled Family.* New York: Basic Books.

Adler, A. (1920). *Praxis und Theorie der Individualpsychologies.* München: Bergmann, 3. Aufl. 1927.

Aichhorn, A. (1925). *Wayward Youth.* London: Putnam, 1936.

Ammon, G. (1973). *Gruppenpsychotherapie.* Hamburg: Hoffmann und Campe.

Angyal, A. (1941). *Foundation for a Science of Personality.* New York: Commonwealth.

Auerbach, A., ed. (1959). *Schizophrenia.* New York: Ronald.

Axline, V. (1947). *Play Therapy.* Boston: Houghton Mifflin.

Balint, M. (1957). *Der Arzt, sein Patient und die Krankheit.* Stuttgart: Klett.

Bandura, A. (1969). *Principles of Behavior Modification*. New York: Holt, Rinehart and Winston.

Bateson, G., Jackson, D. D., Haley, J., and Weakland, J. (1956). Toward a theory of schizophrenia. *Behavioral Science* 1:251–264.

Battegay, R. (1967). *Der Mensch in der Gruppe. II. Allgemeine und Spezielle Gruppentherapeutische Aspekte*. Bern: Huber.

Bell, N. W., and Vogel, E. F., eds. (1960). *A Modern Introduction to the Family*. New York: Free Press.

Berne, E. (1964). *Games People Play*. New York: Grove Press.

Bertalanffy, L. von (1968). *General Systems Theory*. New York: Braziller.

Binswanger, L. (1953). *Grundformen und Erkenntnis Menschlichen Daseins*. Zürich: Niehaus.

Bion, W. R. (1961). *Experiences in Groups*. London: Tavistock.

Bloch, D. A. ed. (1973). *Techniques of Family Therapy: A Primer*. New York: Grune & Stratton.

Blöschl, L. (1969). *Grundlagen und Methoden der Verhaltenstherapie*. Bern: Huber.

Boszormenyi-Nagy, I., and Framo, J. L., eds. (1965). *Intensive Family Therapy: Theoretical and Practical Aspects*. New York: Harper & Row.

Bowen, M. (1959). Family relations in schizophrenia. In *Schizophrenia*, ed. A. Auerbach. New York: Ronald.

_____ (1960). A family concept of schizophrenia. In *The Etiology of Schizophrenia*, ed. D. D. Jackson. New York: Basic Books.

_____ (1965). Family therapy with schizophrenia in the hospital and in private practice. In *Intensive Family Therapy*, ed. I. Boszormenyi-Nagy and J. L. Framo. New York: Harper & Row.

_____ (1971). Family therapy and family group therapy. In *Comprehensive Group Therapy*, ed. H. Kaplan and P. Sadock. Baltimore: Williams & Wilkins.

_____ (1978). *Family Therapy in Clinical Practice.* New York: Jason Aronson.

Bühler, C., and Massarik, F., eds. (1968). *The Course of Human Life.* New York: Springer.

Bühler, K. (1930). *Die Geistige Entwicklung des Kindes.* Jena: G. Fischer.

Caruso, I. A. (1952). *Psychoanalyse und Synthese.* Wien: Herder.

Charcot, J. M. (1886–1890). *Oeuvres Complètes.* Paris: Lecrosnier et Babé.

Chomsky, N. (1957). *Syntactic Structures.* The Hague: Gravenhage.

_____ (1965). *Aspects of the Theory of Syntax.* Cambridge, MA: M.I.T. Press.

Dollard, J., and Miller, N. E. (1950). *Personality and Psychotherapy.* New York: McGraw-Hill.

Ellis. A. (1950). *An Introduction to the Principles of Scientific Psychoanalysis.* Provincetown, MA: Journal Press.

Erikson, E. H. (1950). *Childhood and Society.* New York: W. W. Norton.

_____ (1959). *Identity and the Life Cycle.* New York: International Universities Press.

Eysenck, H. J. (1964). *Experiments in Behavior Therapy.* New York: Pergamon.

Eysenck, H. J., and Rachman, S. (1965). *The Causes and Cures of Neurosis.* London: Routledge and Kegan Paul.

Fairbairn, W. R. D. (1952). *Psychoanalytic Studies of the Personality.* London: Tavistock.

Foulkes, S. H. (1974). *Gruppenanalytische Psychotherapie.* München: Kindler.

Framo, J. L. (1973). Marriage therapy in a couples group. In *Techniques of Family Therapy: A Primer,* ed. D. A. Bloch. New York: Grune & Stratton.

Frankl, V. E. (1947). *Die Existenzanalyse und die Probleme der Zeit.* Wien: Amandus.

Freud, A. (1927). *Einführung in die Technik der Kinderanalyse.* Wien: International Psychoanalytic Verlag.

Freud, S. (1894). Die Abwehr-Neuropsychosen. *Gesammelte Werke,* vol. 1. London: Imago, 1940–1965.

—— (1900). Die Traumdeutung. *Gesammelte Werke,* vol. 2/3. London: Imago, 1940–1965.

—— (1916). Trauer und Melancholie. *Gesammelte Werke,* vol. 10. London: Imago, 1940–1965.

—— (1916–1917). Vorlesungen zur Einführung in die Psychoanalyse. *Gesammelte Werke,* vol. 11. London: Imago, 1940–1965.

—— (1937). Die endliche und die unendliche Analyse. *Gesammelte Werke,* vol. 16. London: Imago, 1940–1965.

Friedmann, A. S. (1965). *Psychotherapy for the Whole Family: Case Histories, Techniques, and Concepts of Family Therapy of Schizophrenia in the Home and Clinic.* New York: Springer.

Fromm-Reichmann, F. (1950). *Principles of Intensive Psychotherapy.* Chicago: University of Chicago Press.

Gerlicher, K. ed. (1977). *Familientherapie in der Erziehungsberatung.* Basel: Beltz.

Glasser, W. (1965). *Reality Therapy.* New York: Harper & Row.

Glick, I. D., and Haley, J. (1971). *Family Therapy and Research.* New York: Grune & Stratton.

Goldstein, K. (1940). *Human Nature in the Light of Psychotherapy.* Cambridge: Harvard University Press.

Gray, W., Duhl, F. J., and Rizzo, N. D., eds. (1969). *General Systems Theory and Psychiatry.* Boston: Little, Brown.

Grinker, R., ed. (1956). *Toward a Unified Theory of Human Behavior.* New York: Basic Books.

Guntrip, H. (1969). *Schizoid Phenomena, Object Relations and the Self.* New York: International Universities Press.

Haley, J. (1963). *Strategies of Psychotherapy.* New York: Grune & Stratton.

Harlow, H. F. (1958). The nature of love. *American Psychologist* 13:673–685.

Harris, T. A. (1967). *I'm O.K. You're O.K.: A Practical Guide to Transactional Analysis.* New York: Harper & Row.

Hart, J. T., and Tomlinson, T. M. (1970). *New Directions in Client-Centered Therapy.* Boston: Houghton Mifflin.

Hilgard, E. R., and Bower, G. H. (1966). *Theories of Learning.* 3rd ed. New York: Meredith.

Hörmann, H. (1970). *Psychologie der Sprache.* 2nd ed. Berlin: Springer.

Hull, C. L. (1943). *Principles of Behavior.* New York: Appleton-Century-Crofts.

Institoris, H., and Sprenger, J. (1487). *Malleus Maleficorum.*

Jackson, D. D. ed. (1960). *Etiology of Schizophrenia.* New York: Basic Books.

Janet, P. (1892). *L'État Mental des Hystériques.* In German. Leipzig: Deuticke, 1894.

Janov, A. (1970). *The Primal Scream.* New York: Dell.

Jaspers, K. (1946). *Allgemeine Psychopathologie.* Berlin: Springer.

Jung. C. G. (1912). Wandlungen und Symbole der Libido. *Gesammelte Werke,* vol. 5. Olten: Walter, 1935–1976.

Kelly, G. A. (1955). *The Psychology of Personal Constructs.* 2 vols. New York: W. W. Norton.

Klein, M. (1932). *The Psychoanalysis of Children.* London: Hogarth.

Kraepelin, E. (1883). *Psychiatrie.* 9th ed. Leipzig: Barth, 1927.

Laing, R. D., Phillipson, H., and Russel, L. (1966). *Interpersonal Perception.* London: Tavistock.

Laqueur, H. P. (1973). Multiple family therapy: questions and answers. In *Techniques of Family Therapy: A Primer,* ed. D. A. Bloch. New York: Grune & Stratton.

Lazarus, A. A. (1971). *Behavior Therapy and Beyond*. New York: McGraw-Hill.

Leuner, H. (1970). *Katathymes Bilderleben*. Stuttgart: Thieme.

Lidz, T., Fleck, S., and Cornelison, A. R. (1965). *Schizophrenia and the Family*. New York: International Universities Press.

London, P. (1972). The end of ideology in behavior modification. *American Journal of Psychology* 27:913–920.

Lorenz, K. (1939). Vergleichende Verhaltensforschung. *Zoologischer Anzeiger Supplement* 12:69–102.

——— (1943). Die angeborenen Formen möglicher Erfahrung. *Zeitschrift für Tierpsychologie* 5:235–409.

——— (1952). *King Solomon's Ring: New Light on Animal Ways*. London: Methuen.

Mahrer, A. R., ed. (1967). *The Goals of Psychotherapy*. New York: Appleton-Century-Crofts.

Mandel, A., Mandel, K. H., Stadter, E., and Zimmer, D. (1971). *Einübung in Partnerschaft durch Kommunikations- und Verhaltenstherapie*. München: Pfeiffer.

Mandel, K. H., Mandel, A., and Rosenthal, H. (1975). *Einübung der Liebesfahigkeit*. München: Pfeiffer.

Maslow, A. H. (1954). *Motivation and Personality*. New York: Harper & Row.

May, R. (1953). *Man's Search for Himself*. New York: W. W. Norton.

Meistermann-Seeger, E. (1976). *Gestörte Familien*. München: Beck.

Meyer, V., and Chesser, E. S. (1970). *Behaviour Therapy in Clinical Psychiatry*. Harmondsworth: Penguin.

Midelfort, C. F. (1957). *The Family in Psychotherapy*. New York: McGraw-Hill.

Minuchin, S. (1974). *Families and Family Therapy*. Cambridge, MA: Harvard University Press.

Moreno, J. L. (1946). *Psychodrama*. New York: Beacon Press.

Mowrer, O. H. (1950). *Learning Theory and Personality Dynamics.* New York: Ronald.

Pakesch, E., ed. (1973). Die Familie als Patient (International Symposium. Graz): Akademische Druck- und Verlagsanstalt, 1974.

Papp, P., ed. (1977). *Family Therapy: Full Length Case Studies.* New York: John Wiley.

Parsons, T. (1951). *The Social System.* New York: Free Press.

Parsons, T., and Bales, R. F. (1955). *Family Socialization and Interaction Process.* New York: Free Press.

Perls, F. (1973). *The Gestalt Approach and Eye Witness to Therapy.* Palo Alto, CA: Science and Behavior Books.

Perls, F., Hefferline, R., and Goodman, P. (1951). *Gestalt Therapy.* New York: Julian Press.

Pongratz, L. J. (1973). *Lehrbuch der Klinischen Psychologie.* Göttingen: Hogrefe.

———— ed. (1978). *Handbuch der Psychologie.* Vol. 8. *Klinische Psychologie.* Göttingen: Hogrefe.

Portmann, A. (1956). *Zoologie und das neue Bild des Menschen.* Hamburg: Rowohlt.

Richter, H. E. (1970). *Patient Familie: Entstehung, Struktur und Therapie von Konflikten in Ehe und Familie.* Hamburg: Rowohlt.

———— (1972). *Die Gruppe.* Hamburg: Rowohlt.

Richter, H. E., Strotzka, H., and Willi, J., eds. (1976). *Familie und seelische Krankheit.* Hamburg: Rowohlt.

Rogers, C. R. (1942). *Client-Centered Therapy.* Boston: Houghton Mifflin, 1951.

Rosen, J. N. (1953). *Direct Analysis.* New York: Grune & Stratton.

Ruesch, J., and Bateson, G. (1951). *Communication, the Social Matrix of Psychiatry.* New York: W. W. Norton.

Satir, V. (1964). *Conjoint Family Therapy.* Rev. ed. Palo Alto: Science and Behavior Books, 1967.

Schraml, W. J., ed. (1970). *Klinische Psychologie.* Bern: Huber.

Schultz, I. H. (1932). *Das autogene Training.* Stuttgart: Thieme, 1950.

Schultz-Hencke, H. (1940). *Der gehemmte Mensch.* Stuttgart: Thieme, 1950.

—— (1951). *Lehrbuch der analytischen Psychotherapie.* Stuttgart: Thieme.

Slavson, S. R. (1950). *Analytic Group Psychotherapy.* New York: Columbia University Press.

Spitz, R. A. (1957). *Die Entstehung der ersten Objektbe-ziehungen.* Stuttgart: Klett.

Stierlin, H. (1975). *Von der Psychoanalyse zur Familientherapie.* Stuttgart: Klett.

Sullivan, H. S. (1947). *Conception of Modern Psychiatry.* Washington, DC: William Alanson White Foundation.

Tausch, R. (1968). *Gesprächspsychotherapie.* Göttingen: Hogrefe.

Tinbergen, N. (1951). *The Study of Instinct.* Oxford: Clarendon Press.

—— (1953). *Social Behavior in Animals, with Special Reference to Vertebrates.* London: Methuen.

Tolman, E. C. (1932). *Purposive Behavior in Animals and Men.* New York: Century.

Toman, W. (1959a). Die Familienkonstellation und ihre psychologische Bedeutung. *Psychologische Rundschau* 10:1–15.

—— (1959b). Family constellation as a basic personality determinant. *Journal of Individual Psychology* 15:199–211.

—— (1961). *Family constellation.* 3rd rev. ed. New York: Springer, 1976.

—— (1965). *Familienkonstellationen.* 2nd rev. ed. München: Beck, 1974.

—— (1968). *Motivation, Persönlichkeit, Umwelt.* Göttingen: Hogrefe.

—— (1971). The "duplication theorem" of social relationships as tested in the general population. *Psychological Review* 78:380–390.

_____ (1977). Familientherapie im Kontext der Psychotherapie. In *Familientherapie in der Erziehungsberatung*, ed. K. Gerlicher. Weinheim: Beltz.

_____ (1978a). Ziele der Psychotherapie. In *Handbuch der Psychologie*, vol. 8/2, 1820–1830. Göttingen: Hogrefe.

_____ (1978b). *Tiefenpsychologie*. Stuttgart: Kohlhammer.

_____ (1979). *Familientherapie: Grundlagen, empirische Erkenntnisse und Praxis*. Darmstadt: Wissenschaftliche Buchgesellschaft.

Toman, W., and Preiser, S. (1973). *Familienkonstellationen und ihre Störungen*. Stuttgart: Enke.

Watzlawick, P., Beavin, J. H., and Jackson, D. D. (1967). *Pragmatics of Human Communication: A Study of Interactional Patterns, Pathologies and Paradoxes*. New York: W. W. Norton.

Weizsäcker, V. von (1947a). *Körpergeschehen und Neurose*. Stuttgart: Klett.

_____ (1947b). *Der Gestaltkreis*. Stuttgart: Klett.

Whitaker, C. A., and Malone, T. P. (1953). *The Roots of Psychotherapy*. New York: McGraw-Hill.

Winnicott, D. W. (1965). *The Maturational Processes and the Facilitating Environment*. London: Hogarth.

Wolberg, L. R. (1948). *Medical Hypnosis*. 2 vols. New York: Grune & Stratton.

Wolpe, J. (1958). *Psychotherapy by Reciprocal Inhibition*. Stanford, CA: Stanford University Press.

Wolpe, J., and Lazarus, A. A. (1966). *Behaviour Therapy Techniques*. New York: Pergamon.

Wynne, L. C., Rykoff, I., Day, J., et al. (1960). Pseudomutualization in the family relations of schizophrenics. In *A Modern Introduction to the Family*, ed. N. W. Bell and E. Vogel. New York: Free Press.

Yalom, B. (1970). *Theory and Practice of Group Psychotherapy.* New York: Basic Books.

Yates, A. J. (1970). *Behavior Therapy.* New York: John Wiley.

Zilboorg, G., and Henry, G. W. (1941). *A History of Medical Psychology.* New York: W. W. Norton.

SUBJECT INDEX

A

Abstinence, of psychotherapist,
6–7, 29, 110–111, 113,
129–137, 202–205
Acting out, 22
Activity phase of childhood,
74–75
  regression to, 101
Adolescence, 80–82
Age-rank conflict of sibling roles,
47–48, 49–50
Ambivalence over loss, 67, 96
Anal phase of childhood, 74–75
  regression to, 101
Anxiety, inhibition of, 10
Autogenic training, 10

B

Behavior therapy, 9–11, 109

C

Case histories of family therapy,
139–166, 168–192, 213–219
Catathymic imagery, 13
Characteristics of children,
  constitutional, 25–26, 61–62
  innate, 61–62
  mental, 45–46, 79
  physical, 45–46
Child configurations, 40
  complex, 43–46
  single, 40, 60–61
Child therapy, 8, 17–18
Childhood
  early, 72–77
  late, 77–79
Classical psychotherapy, 5–8, 10,
202–205
Client-centered therapy, 8–9, 109
Compatibility or complementarity

235

AUTHOR INDEX

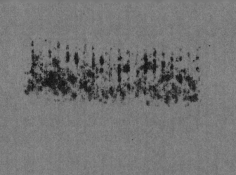

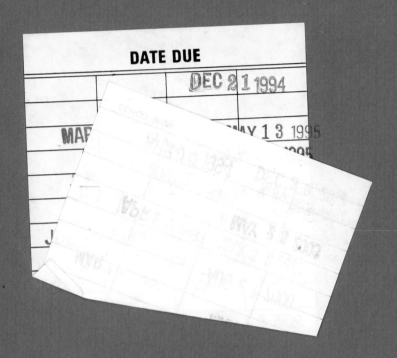